A Stillness in the Pines

The Commonwealth Fund Book Program
gratefully acknowledges
the assistance of the Rockefeller University
in the administration of the program.

overleaf: red-cockaded woodpecker

A Stillness in the Pines

THE ECOLOGY OF THE
RED-COCKADED WOODPECKER

ROBERT W. McFARLANE

Illustrations by
ELLEN MABRY

A volume of
THE COMMONWEALTH FUND BOOK PROGRAM
under the editorship of LEWIS THOMAS, M.D.

W·W·NORTON & COMPANY
New York · London

Copyright © 1992 by the Commonwealth Fund Book Program
All rights reserved.

Printed in the United States of America.

The text of this book is composed in Goudy Old Style,
with the display set in Book Jacket Italic.
Composition and manufacturing by the Haddon Craftsmen, Inc.
Book design by Jacques Chazaud

First Edition

Library of Congress Cataloging-in-Publication Data
McFarlane, Robert W.
A stillness in the pines : the ecology of the red-cockaded woodpecker /
Robert W. McFarlane ; illustrations by Ellen Mabry.
p.   cm.—(The Commonwealth Fund Book Program)
Includes bibliographical references and index.
1. Red-cockaded woodpecker.   2. Red-cockaded woodpecker—Southern
States—Effect of habitat modification on.   3. Birds, Protection
of—Southern States.   4. Rare birds—Southern States.   5. Endangered
species—Southern States.   6. Loblolly pine—Southern
States—Ecology.   7. Extinction (Biology)   I. Series: Commonwealth
Fund Book Program (Series)
QL696.P56M44   1992 333.95′8—dc20   91–2771

ISBN 0–393–03066–0

W. W. Norton & Company, Inc., 500 Fifth Avenue, New York, N.Y. 10110
W. W. Norton & Company, Ltd., 10 Coptic Street, London WC1A 1PU

1 2 3 4 5 6 7 8 9 0

This book is dedicated to

Dan Lay
and
David Ligon
*who first recognized the plight of
the red-cockaded woodpecker*

Jerry Jackson
who forged a recovery plan amongst recalcitrants

Dick Conner
who dared to bell the tiger

and

Judge Robert Parker
who pulled the tiger's teeth.

Contents

7

CONTENTS

List of Figures

Foreword

UNTIL A LITTLE more than a hundred years ago there stretched a great, predominantly pine forest from Texas through the Deep South to Virginia. This wilderness, broken only by rivers and the occasional hand-hewn clearing, had among its many natural inhabitants a species of pine beetle and a voracious feeder on pine beetles aptly known to ornithology as the red-cockaded woodpecker. The pine beetle (to the dismay of the timber industry) still flourishes in the little that remains of the forest, but the red-cockaded woodpecker has been added to the ever-growing list of endangered species. Indeed, it is close to extinction. The decline of the red-cockaded woodpecker, which has been encouraged at every turn by the stubbornly misguided hand of man, is the subject of Robert W. McFarlane's book. But *A Stillness in the Pines* has a thrust much broader than that. In leading us toward an understanding of the nature and needs of the red-cockaded woodpecker, its habitat and feeding and breeding requirements, its place in the great biological chain, it also leads us from microcosm to macrocosm, from ecosystem to an appreciation of the fundamental science of ecology.

Several years ago the Commonwealth Fund decided at the suggestion of its president, Margaret E. Mahoney, to sponsor a Book Program in which working scientists of distinction were invited to write about their work for a literate lay audience. Dr. McFarlane—a biologist equally at home in the field, in the laboratory, and in the university lecture hall—is such a scientist, and the Book Program is pleased to offer his book as its sixth publication.

The advisory committee for the Commonwealth Fund Book Program, which recommended the sponsorship of this book, consists of the following members: Lewis Thomas, M.D., director; Alexander C. Bearn, M.D., deputy director; Lynn Margulis, Ph.D.; Maclyn McCarty, M.D., Lady Medawar; Berton Roueché; Frederick Seitz, Ph.D.; and Otto Westphal, M.D. The publisher is represented by Edwin Barber, director of the Trade Department at W. W. Norton & Company, Inc. Jan Maier is administrative assistant.

BERTON ROUECHÉ

Prologue

THIS BOOK BEGAN as musings about death. Not the death of an individual—all creatures have a relatively well-known limit to their existence on earth—but the death of a biological species. Extinction, a topic which has achieved some prominence in our technological era, as species disappear at an ever-increasing rate. A number of species have dwindled to a relative handful of individuals, now threatened by the vagaries of nature: an unseasonal storm; the unpredictable flowering of bamboo plants; the ignorance of uncaring humans. Other species of concern remain abundant. It is difficult to conceive of 1 million African elephants as endangered. Yet the trends are clear, and the clash between humans and elephants competing for common resources seems inevitable. The elephant population has recently shrunk from 5 million to 700,000 in only a dozen years, accelerated by a human lust for ivory. A century ago few people thought the millions of American bison would ever stand on the brink of extinction, but they survive today only in a handful of protected herds.

The creature that gave rise to this book is neither as familiar nor as large and conspicuous as some other endangered animals. It does not undertake arduous semiannual migrations between breeding and wintering grounds like the whooping crane. It does not migrate at all. Nor does it reward an observer with awe-inspiring stoops upon its targeted prey, as the peregrine falcon does, or flashy tactics and acts of piracy, as the bald eagle does. It is a predator, without doubt, but only spiders, centipedes, millipedes, and other jointed-legged creatures fear its appearance.

The casual bird watcher or enthusiastic life lister need not travel to exotic lands (by most standards, at least) to glimpse this denizen of the pinewoods. Members of this species inhabit an area more than a thousand miles across the southern tier of states, from Texas to Virginia. But neither can you expect to find it in the first pine grove you come across in this area. You will spot its close relatives, without doubt, but you are unlikely to glimpse this elusive species. Not that it is at all shy or wary. It is quite at home in towns and city parks, even college campuses. It will nest right next to a busy highway on occasion. It can be alternately conspicuous and evasive, often difficult to observe even when you know exactly where to look. Rare in numbers? That is a subjective judgment, depending upon your viewpoint. Difficult to census under any circumstances, it presently numbers no fewer than three thousand birds and perhaps as many as nine thousand. Is it really endangered? This is a fair, and critical, question. Seemingly not, until you examine its recent history and note its shrinking range, decline in numbers, and disappearing habitat. So how many birds constitute a stable population, enough to guarantee its continued existence? Here is another important question, one difficult to answer, particularly if you seek consensus. Why is this species going extinct? What can be done? What is being done? What is this creature?

Our disappearing bird is the red-cockaded woodpecker, an eight-inch, zebra-striped, black-and-white woodpecker found only in the pinewoods of the southeastern United States. It is a specialist competing in a world of generalists, a featherweight thrown headlong into the path of giant economic and management forces, clogging up the machinery, thanks to the Endangered Species Act. Neither majestic of itself nor rare enough to arouse the ire of spirited supporters, it is besieged on all sides by timber beasts, exploitive managers, and shortsighted politicians.

To understand this species and its plight, we must turn from musings about death to questions concerning life. Death is imminent from the moment of conception, held abeyant only by continual satisfaction of the requisites for life. Species must adapt and evolve with changing environmental conditions or succumb ignominiously to extinction, perhaps bequeathing to the world a few faint impressions in the mud to excite and confound the descendants of a distant species, screening their dirtpile in search of paleontological diamonds.

Science, from one perspective, is the art of phrasing questions and identifying their attendant assumptions. Its basic tenet is that nature has no secrets. The obstacles to furthering knowledge lie in formulating the right questions and in circumventing ambiguous answers, never an easy task. The best practitioners know that incisive questions and skillful analysis will ultimately yield their reward. Artful questions may require new technology, often from unrelated disciplines. New questions may require fresh insight, unencumbered by the baggage of past experience, and a probing mind to test old concepts. The importance of the proper question is often overlooked, by experienced observer and novice alike.

It is my intention to explore the process of extinction by posing questions about life. What facets of the world about it are important to a red-cockaded woodpecker? Which of these are critical? Are we seeking answers in the wrong places? Can we ever view the world from the perspective of a woodpecker, or any other species? To do this, we must expand our horizon far beyond woodpeckers.

We must examine how nature is assembled and how the pieces fit and function together. We must seek out the patterns that exist in the natural world. It is nowadays a common experience, in this era of near-instant travel, for a biologist to arrive suddenly on a continent new to his experience and strangely feel quite at home. Plants growing in similar climates and soil seem to produce similar life-forms. Animals exploiting similar plants, though continents apart, develop similar life-styles and haunting resemblances to their biological counterparts elsewhere, despite blood relationships that grow vanishingly small. Do these mimics arise when creatures unknowingly play the same evolutionary game, following unseen but pervasive rules to similar conclusions?

All animals must acquire certain minimal resources to exist. First, they must eat. Seemingly obvious, this requirement is nonetheless primal. Failure to obtain sufficient nutrients guarantees quick extinction. Next, they must have shelter of some kind. For some, it is perhaps needed only at critical junctures in their life. For others, shelter is a near-constant requirement. While food serves to fuel internal metabolic needs, shelter ameliorates the harsh environment. It may provide concealment from predators, regulate internal body temperature, or sporadically aid in passage through an environmental "crunch" when conditions become hazardous to life. But shelter seems necessary for all creatures at some stage in their lives.

Our third component of survival is really a special combination of the first two, the unique food and shelter requirements needed for successful reproduction. Individuals may find sufficient food and shelter to survive, but unless they reproduce successfully, the species will almost certainly die. Reproduction may involve special shelter needs to hide eggs or young or particular dietary requirements.

Food and shelter are rarely, if ever, unlimited resources. As populations grow, limited resources restrict population growth, and individuals of the same and differing species begin to compete. Competition as a guiding force in evolution is an elegant concept and readily imagined. Successful competitors persist while less able individuals, and species, perish. Detecting competition and measuring competitive advantages are terribly difficult. Even demonstrating that competition truly exists is no simple task.

As more and more species crowd into a given habitat, the possibilities for competitive jostling increase. How many species can be packed into a given environment? How do habitats with many species differ from habitats with few species? What kinds of species are most compatible? What are the rules for assembling animal communities?

History has taught us there are innumerable routes to extinction. Some are swift; others, imperceptibly slow. When can the process be reversed? How can man the expediter become man the intervener? Can Western man the developer become a caretaker, make peace with nature, and save his own species as well?

My goal is to explore some of the ground rules by which the game of life is played. As we seek to understand the interconnectedness of the natural world, we will experience the challenge of exploring nature's mysteries and reap the rewards that await the persistent interrogator.

The Third Dimension

FROM EASTERN TEXAS the remnants of a once-magnificent forest, nurtured by moisture from the Gulf of Mexico, extends a thousand miles to the Atlantic shore and as far north as the Chesapeake Bay. The coastal plain of the Gulf states and the Florida peninsula are clothed with an evergreen forest of conifers and broadleaved hardwood trees. It differs from the tropical rainforests of lower latitudes in having fewer species of trees and shorter trees, many with small, leathery leaves. But the humid, subtropical climate fosters the growth of epiphytes and lianas. Tree trunks and branches are often festooned with mosses, algae, bromeliads, and—that trademark of the Deep South—Spanish moss. Once a continuous continental forest, punctuated only by the Mississippi and lesser rivers, it now persists as scattered islands of remnant replacement trees. This unique woodland gave birth to two woodpeckers, one large and one small, each with distinct needs for survival. Today the largest is gone and the other is struggling.

In this region of gentle slopes, sluggish, meandering blackwater streams, and numerous marshes, swamps, and lakes, the vegetation changes abruptly with very slight shifts in elevation. Desiccation-resistant needleleaf pine trees, especially the longleaf and slash pines, cover the low, sandy ridges that barely retain moisture. Farther downhill, where flatlands retain standing water for much of the year, graceful cypress trees proliferate as evolutionary fence straddlers, bearing cones at the tips of needle boughs, but shedding their needles with the approach of winter. Between these dry-loving and water-loving extremes lies the evergreen oak and magnolia forest. The borders interweave repeatedly. Water-loving cypress trees cling tenuously to eroding stream beds, pushing upstream as far as groundwater seepage will permit. Erosion-resistant patches of soil protrude a mere foot above the floodplain, barely noticeable to the traveler except for the incongruous stand of pines doggedly persisting on their marooned islet.

At higher elevations farther inland grows a mixed forest of many species: the deciduous broadleaf oaks, hickories, sweetgum, beech, red maple, and elm interspersed with needleleaf evergreen southern "yellow pines," particularly the loblolly and shortleaf species. In many areas at least half the trees in a stand are pines. This mixed pine-hardwood forest represents the final stage of plant succession, the climax forest, for this region. Plant species succeed one another in an orderly fashion as plant communities develop. Pine trees, able to withstand full sunlight and dry conditions for extended periods, are among the first trees to establish themselves in this climate. But once established, pine forests have unwittingly sown the seeds of their own destruction. Hardwood trees flourish in the shade of the tall pines, which permit sufficient light for hardwood growth to filter down between their tenuous needles. But the broad leaves of the hardwood trees block out so much light that pines can no longer sprout and prosper in the deep shade of their deciduous neighbors. Young pines of all ages are common in pine stands, creating the replacement generation, growing slowly until large trees succumb to old age or disease and fall. When hardwood trees dominate the understory of the woods and eventually come to form the bulk of the canopy, the replacement pines are rare, spindly, and widely scattered.

Yet pure or nearly pure pine stands can be found. How can this be? The answer involves another natural phenomenon—fire. Pines have evolved excellent countermeasures against fire damage. Rapid growth raises the needle-bearing branches above the forest floor, where fire presents the greatest danger. Thick insulating bark protects the thin growing layer of living cells, the cambium, from the heat of the blaze, emerging with trunks black and ugly but still alive. Cones protect the seeds of the new generation for extended periods before releasing them, perhaps to a desolate, fire-blackened landscape below. When fire does come, either from lightning bolt or from humans, the litter of dry pine needles burns quickly, and the fire moves on, frequently leaving the canopy unscathed. Not so with the deciduous hardwood trees. Growing slowly, remaining close to the ground for many years, and lacking the protective bark, the young hardwoods fail to survive the ravages of the fire. Once again pines can sprout and receive nourishment from the ashes of their former competitors. The pines have received a new lease on life and may persist for many years as fire iterations create a pine-dominated, fire-maintained, subclimax forest and repeatedly short-circuit the succession process.

Hardwood trees, growing slowly, do not yield an adequate economic return from the perspective of foresters and are therefore deemed undesirable. After decades of assiduously stomping out every forest fire that sprang forth, and losing the battle for dominance between desirable pines and the detested hardwoods, foresters have reeducated Smokey the Bear. They have trained him to set controlled burns that eliminate hardwood growth and reduce the amount of leaf and needle litter on the ground, thereby limiting the amount of fuel available to feed wildfires. The pure pine stands we now encounter are most often the result of natural reforestation of lands logged long ago, or abandoned agricultural land, or pine plantations created in the pursuit of the newest cash crop, the wood fiber needed to feed our insatiable demand for paper.

The forest of this subtropical ecological region is inhabited by a rich and diverse community of animals, including more than three hundred species of birds. A prominent component of this avifauna is an assemblage of nine species of woodpeckers, more than any other forest in North America. Most of these woodpeckers live throughout the continent, successfully inhabiting a number of ecological regions. Only two of these species, the ivory-billed woodpecker and the red-cockaded woodpecker, are restricted to this ecoregion. These are also the only two woodpeckers threatened with extinction. The ivory-billed woodpecker has been recognized as endangered for nearly a hundred years, was considered extinct in the late 1920s before a few survivors were discovered, and probably has passed the point of no return. Nobody has validated any observations of this species for a decade. The smaller red-cockaded woodpecker, always more abundant than the ivory-billed, may still exist in adequate numbers to reverse its shrinking trend, if we can identify and correct the causes of its decline.

What regulates the number of bird species that can inhabit a given ecosystem? Over the past thirty years ornithologists have come to realize that the physical structure of the habitat sets limits on the number of cohabiting avian species. To create any terrestrial community, we must begin with plants.

They alone can capture the extraterrestrial energy of sunlight and delay the inevitable decay of that energy to heat, using the energy for their own purposes in the interval. Animals cannot exist on bare earth, for there is nothing for them to feed upon. Green plants alone form the basis of any significant ecological food web. The plants which can exist at a given spot on the surface of the globe are dependent upon the climate and the raw material available for the formation of soil.

Except for the Mississippi floodplain and delta, which are rich with topsoil from the heartland of America, the soils of this southeastern ecoregion, whether young or old, are poor in nutrients. Some scientists would say, only half in jest, that compared with the continental prairies, this forested land has no soil at all. The forest was sparing of the scant nutrients it possessed. They dropped gently to the ground as fallen leaves and needles over extended periods of time. This nutrient wealth collected in the rich humus and deep organic litter and was quickly recycled back to the treetops. The forest hoarded moisture, nurturing the hidden world of shredding and chewing creatures that inhabited the dark interface between the earth and the air, creating soil with the few resources available.

Europeans changed all that. As trees fell and dwellings rose, the land was exposed to the sun, denuded, turned upside down with stick and wooden plow. New crops thrust their roots into the sparse soil and thrived for a few years. But the crops were removed from the ecosystem when harvested, and the nourishing humus disappeared. Pelting rain etched deep gullies up the hillsides as topsoil marched to the sea. Stripped of its nutrients and abandoned by the farmers, the land slowly began to sprout the only crop it was ever meant to grow—trees.

Given a tough, pioneering plant able to withstand direct sunlight, wind, and desiccation, such as a grass or other small herb, a plant community can establish itself. Let us assume that the first plant soon spreads and covers the entire surface of the ground. By itself it has created what is essentially a two-dimensional habitat. The plants are occupying extensive horizontal space but virtually no vertical dimension, a few short roots, a few short stems, and little else. This is sufficient, however, to change the microhabitat within and beneath the plants. Temperature extremes of the shaded earth are lessened. As the grass grows and dies, it creates fodder for the ubiquitous decomposer organisms that recycle the plant nutrients back to the soil. In fact, a few nutrients, extracted by the plants from air and water in one chemical form and transformed with the aid of enzyme magic into new molecular structures, may not have previously existed. But most important, it has provided the basis for an animal community. Jointed-legged arthropods will be the first to invade the new habitat, soon followed by reptiles, birds, and mammals in pursuit of the invertebrates.

Few birds eat grass stems and leaves directly. In this grassland habitat, birds exist by pursuing the abundant insects or consuming the nutrient-rich seeds produced by the plants. These birds will typically have slender, pointed bills to facilitate the capture of insects or short, stout bills mechanically capable of cracking tough seed coats. Species such as meadowlarks and sparrows construct their nests at the base of bunched vegetation and frequently build an overhead dome to conceal the eggs and incubating adults. Thus birds frequenting such a habitat will be insect-eaters or seedeaters, or both, and nest on the surface of the ground.

The biological community we have described is a very simple one: a single species of grass; a few arthropods that function either as primary consumers, eating the grass directly, or secondary consumers, bypassing the grass but eating those animals that did eat the grass; and a few birds that consume

FIGURE 1-1 Insectivorous (meadowlark, below) and granivorous (dickcissel, above) birds typical of grasslands.

the seeds or the arthropods, or both. Such a simple community is rare in nature, generally found only under adverse environmental conditions, for example, in areas of extreme aridity or temperatures or in areas poisoned by toxic chemicals.

Usually we find a more diverse mixture of coexisting species. Other grasses and herbs will find a vacant niche and perform some facet of living a little differently, or a little better, and succeed in coexisting with the established vegetation. As plant diversity increases, arthropod diversity will follow, and specialization will evolve. Five or six species of birds may be able to coexist in such an environment as they exploit various resources for food and reproduction. But life on this grassland is still two-dimensional, particularly for the birds. They can still feed only on and among the grasses and other herbs and nest only on the ground.

As individual plants reproduce and come to occupy all the available space, a limited resource, they must launch out in new directions. As plants are crowded together, they begin to shade one another, and sunlight, heretofore an unlimited resource, is no longer equally available to all. A plant can compete for scarce nutrients by spreading the breadth and depth of its root system, poaching on its neighbors' turf. But the solution to restricted sunlight is to grow upward and intercept the rays of sunlight before a neighboring plant gets them. Growing skyward is one thing, but staying there is quite another. Tall grasses are susceptible to stem breakage unless masses of plants grow close together, supporting one another. An alternative is to incorporate strong woody tissue into the stems. From a single, well-anchored origin at the ground, one or more strong woody stems can develop vertically and laterally into the configuration we know as a shrub.

The vertical development of a plant community has lasting effects on its animal inhabitants. Tall grasses growing close together impede movement and restrict observation of approaching predators. Birds that live in such vegetation tend to have short wings and tails and move on the ground over, under, and around the grass stems rather than attempt flight in such a dense environment. Birders hear these species more often than they see them and have great difficulty flushing them.

Shrubs affect the animal communities even more. Because shrubs have developed tough, woody stems and branches for support, not all parts are equally edible to plant-eaters. Growing higher above the ground up into desiccating winds, shrubs may develop tough leaf surfaces to curtail evaporation. Arthropods must then develop new strategies. Mouthparts that readily demolish tender plants quickly flounder when attacking tough bark and leaves. Since the shrubs, which represent an entirely new food and reproduction resource, may not be close together, the ability to fly from shrub to shrub becomes more important.

New life-style opportunities have arisen for birds as well. Shrubs provide perches and flycatching becomes a viable endeavor. Birds can sit quietly on exposed limbs and watch for flying insects while expending little energy. Sallying forth to capture a flying insect requires a modified bill structure, such as a wider mouth with a more efficient flat, broad bill. The limbs and branches of shrubs, with leaves restricted to the sunlit extremities, also create a new "domed" structure. Small birds can hop from limb to limb within the dome, gleaning insects from limbs and leaves while staying hidden from predators. Small, pointed bills are best for such foraging. The domes also provide an ideal site for nests. Getting the nest and its contents off the ground appears to be a major advantage for most birds, providing a drier and cooler shaded location that predators are less apt to discover.

The density of the shrubs greatly influences the character of the habitat. A few shrubs widely scattered will permit coexistence of grasses and shrubs, hence grass- and shrub-inhabiting birds as well. Abundant, closely spaced shrubs shade surface plants growing beneath them, and some species will be

eliminated. Animals directly or indirectly dependent on the disappearing plants will be affected. Shade-tolerant grasses will persist, but their density and volume will never equal those of grasses growing in full sunlight; thus they will harbor fewer insects and produce fewer seeds. Patches of bare soil may become a prominent feature of the surface once again, particularly beneath the shrubs. The dominant shrubs have permanently changed their environment and its associated animals.

Thus we see that the addition of a third dimension, the vertical growth of plants, can add diversity to an ecosystem by providing new resources for food and reproduction. Animals exploit the surface layer of vegetation or the shrub layer, or both. A combination of surface and shrub vegetation will provide resources for more species of animals than either vegetative type could support alone.

The competition for sunlight will continue. Plants which evolve stronger, taller stems, even to the point of abandoning lower limbs which languish in the shade, will be most successful in garnering sunlight. Broad, woody trunks and deep, thick roots will be necessary to support the superstructure in the wind. We call the resultant profile, a slender vertical trunk supporting a crown of limbs and leaves, a tree. When trees grow close together, with their crowns in near or actual contact, an overhead canopy forms, and a forest begins to take shape.

The formation of this third layer of vegetation, the canopy, in some respects resembles a shrub layer raised above the ground. But important differences determine which animals can utilize the upper layer. Trees, when mature, are typically much larger than shrubs. The limbs are thicker and farther apart, and the crowns are much broader. Leaves are usually concentrated near the ends of limbs, creating open spaces

FIGURE 1-2 Flycatching (scissor-tailed flycatcher, above) and gleaning (Carolina wren, below) birds.

within the crowns, and birds are now able to fly into, out of, and within these spacious crowns. Treetops are accessible to larger birds whereas shrubs are not. All sorts of surface predators are able to climb and clamber about in shrubs, but only animals with special climbing skills gain access to tree crowns. Thus nests in trees are less vulnerable to predators than are nests on the ground or in shrubs. Trees with wider trunks also have greater trunk surface area, which represents a new habitat for arthropods both on and beneath the surface. This, in turn, creates new feeding opportunities for insect-eating predators.

The addition of shrub and tree layers of vegetation in a habitat creates a third vertical dimension in habitat cover that allows arthropods, birds, and other animals to increase in abundance and diversity. The shrub and tree layers provide additional food resources, protective cover from predators and inclement weather, and superior nesting sites. Trees also provide another, less appreciated resource—the trunk, or bole, of the tree itself.

The bark of the tree trunk protects the vital cambium inside. The bark may be thin or thick, with a smooth surface or deep fissures. Alone it provides an important microhabitat exploited by ants and spiders and myriad crawling creatures. But arthropods that are able to penetrate the bark gain access to the cambial tissue and its sweet nutritious juices. It is an excellent nursery for beetle eggs and developing larvae, which tunnel their way in eternal darkness, progressing as far as they can eat. This is how the trunks of trees represent a new foraging ground for those species equipped to exploit it.

For birds, the shift from walking on the ground to hopping onto the limbs of shrubs and tree canopies may have been relatively easy. The body is still horizontal and must balance over its center of gravity. If a bird has one or more hind toes that can oppose the action of the front toes, a minor modification of the toes to provide complete bending results in a firm grip encircling a limb. Perching on a tilted branch can be accommodated by raising one leg higher than the other. Balance is maintained by positioning the body directly above the toes, a difficult feat in strong winds.

Perching on a vertical tree trunk poses a different problem. The center of gravity of a bird's body is suspended in midair, constantly responding to the law of gravity, which insists that such a posture cannot be maintained. It is no longer a matter of balance but one of hanging on.

Man, whose primate ancestors abandoned their arboreal habits many millions of years ago, has secondarily solved the problem of ascending a vertical tree trunk. The first attempt was to shinny up the tree, clasping the trunk with both arms and legs. This is painfully awkward and slow, the advance being one hitch at a time, with the threat of a swift, abrasive descent at any moment of weakness. It is easy to see that treetops are not our natural habitat.

Given a slight advantage, like the variations in the trunk surface found on a coconut palm, and perhaps a slight tilt to the trunk, we can employ a better technique. Picture the bold tropical native, sarong tucked into waistband, bare feet planted on the trunk, arms outstretched with only the hands grasping the trunk, rapidly ascending to the top of the tree. Opposite hands and feet work in unison, providing equal force from each side, and the faster one goes, the easier it is to climb. The feet grab the trunk better when you lean back away from the tree, rather than clasp the trunk to the bosom.

Technological man improved this technique as he began to plant miles of "artificial trees" across the landscape. He cut down tall pines, stripped them of limbs and bark, and impregnated them with foul-tasting, smelly creosote to discourage wood-boring beetles and decomposers. Affixing horizontal arms to their tops, he planted these rehabilitated trees in long rows, festooned them with glass and ceramic insulators, and strung them with endless shining wires. To ascend these modern trees, a person attaches spiked climbing irons to the feet and lower limbs. Jabbing the spikes into the tree trunk offsets

31

the vertical pull of gravity. A broad belt encircles both person and pole to overcome the outward force that strives to separate the person from the pole. The novice climber soon learns that the fastest way to climb successfully is to dig in the spikes, trust the belt, and lean as far back as he or she dares, angling the axis of the body to the pole. Decreasing or eliminating this angle by grasping the pole with both arms guarantees a rapid and startling descent.

Birds yielded manipulating forelimbs in exchange for the power of flight and became the envy of man. Mythology and history are filled with the dreams of men yearning to fly, although they seldom appear willing to yield their opposable fingers in exchange. Many artistic impressions render the wings of angels and other aerialists as a third pair of appendages, a very difficult trick for vertebrates to perform. Exploiting the new vertical resource that tree trunks represent while equipped with a single pair of grasping limbs has proved to be quite a challenge, and only a few birds have succeeded. Several different strategies have worked, however, as we shall see in the next chapter.

At this point you might well inquire if the tree trunk is all that important to birds. After all, the crowns of the trees provide the twigs and leaves that attract the insects that most birds prey upon. In addition, woodpeckers do not spend all their time on tree trunks. Two convincing pieces of evidence suggest that tree trunks are critical to woodpeckers. First, desert areas typically lack trees, or trees that do exist are short, scrubby, and often thorny. The branches extend down the trunk to nearly ground level. In some deserts surrogate trees exist in the form of saguaro and organ-pipe cacti. The Gila woodpecker is quite content to utilize the "trunk" of the saguaro or organ-pipe as a nest site. The smaller ladderbacked woodpecker uses the saguaro and the flowering stalks

FIGURE 1-3 The three-point stance of a utility-pole climber and downy woodpecker (inset).

32

of yucca and agave. These vertical structures are acting as tree trunks without crowns and serve quite well as nest sites for the two woodpeckers. Second, in grasslands or agricultural areas several species of woodpeckers nest in the wooden utility poles, former tree trunks, which arc for miles across these open habitats. The woodpeckers can cause extensive damage to the poles, and utility companies have spent a lot of money to develop impregnable poles and effective repellents, so far with little success. In both instances we see that the availability of a vertical trunk has permitted the woodpeckers, still dependent upon a cavity for nesting, to expand and persist in areas which essentially lack trees.

Thus shrubs and treetops contribute an important third dimension to habitat structure. Moreover, tree trunks provide an important new habitat feature to species that successfully exploit it.

CHAPTER TWO

What Is a Woodpecker?

VERY FEW BIRDS have successfully exploited the opportunities represented by a vertical tree trunk. The nearly 250 types of perching songbirds indigenous to temperate North America constitute the most numerous and diverse group of birds on the continent. Yet of these many species, only 6 make use of tree trunks for climbing and foraging. The best known of these songbird trunk foragers are the 4 species of nuthatches—small, chunky birds with straight, spikelike bills. All nuthatches have very short tails that barely extend beyond the tips of their folded wings and large feet with strong, curved claws. Each has a typical perching foot with three toes pointing forward and a single toe pointing to the rear. Their large toes and claws and small body size permit nuthatches to maintain a strong grip on the tree bark from almost any orientation, head up, sideways, even head down. They move busily along the trunks and branches of trees, gleaning insects and spiders from the surface and crevices in the bark, frequently dangling upside down beneath limbs of trees to do so. They grip the tree solely with their feet, and their tails have no role in their agility. They are most commonly seen perched on tree trunks sideways, with the uppermost leg and foot providing the grip and the lowermost leg serving as a prop.

We find the most unlikely trunk forager among the wood warblers. Most of the 47 species of wood warblers in the United States glean insects from the leaves and twigs of trees, while a few species forage on the ground and in low shrubs. The black-and-white warbler, however, gathers its bug and spider prey principally from the trunks and large limbs of the trees. Like the nuthatches, it has large toes and strong claws, and although its tail is longer than that of nuthatches, it also has no role in clinging to the tree trunks. This warbler tends not to hang upside down or beneath limbs as nuthatches do.

The sixth trunk-foraging songbird in the United States is the brown creeper. The anatomy and behavior of this bird are tailored for trunk foraging. It has short legs and large feet, its long bill is slender and slightly decurved, for probing into bark crevices, and its tail is considerably longer than that of nuthatches or the warbler. Nuthatch tails are about half as long as the length of their folded wing (what we perceive as wing length when the bird is perched with wings folded), black-and-white warbler tails are about two-thirds as long, while the tail feathers of the brown creeper are fully as long as the folded wing. Moreover, the tail feathers of the warbler and nuthatches are symmetrical and square-tipped or just slightly rounded. By contrast, the tail feathers of the creeper

FIGURE 2-1 Treetrunk-foraging songbirds: black-and-white warbler (above), brown creeper (below, left), and nuthatch (below, right).

are asymmetrical in that the outer vane is much narrower than the inner vane, and the tips are sharply pointed. The feathers are relatively stiff, and the tail acts as a prop, providing support to the bird when it is in a vertical, head-up position. The creeper now has three contact points with the tree trunk, its two feet and the tip of its tail.

Besides attaching itself to the tree trunk in a unique manner, the creeper forages differently. It starts at the base of the tree trunk and ascends in short hitches, spiraling up the tree sideways as it painstakingly investigates all crevices for prey. Once it reaches the top, the creeper then flies to the bottom of the trunk of another tree nearby and repeats the process. It rarely indulges in the acrobatic head-down postures of the nuthatches.

This climbing practice saves energy. A tree trunk forager can choose from four strategies. It could begin near the bottom of a tree trunk and proceed upward or at the top of the tree and work its way downward. It could also work bottom to top on one tree and top to bottom on the next but no known species of bird uses this technique. Only birds that glean insect prey from leaves and twigs commonly use the final strategy: following a horizontal foraging path from tree to tree. This last course is efficient for birds foraging the broad treetop but would be wasteful for trunk foragers, which could explore only a short segment of the trunk before moving to another tree. A thorough search for prey hiding in bark crevices or beneath the bark involves vertical, rather than horizontal, movement.

Creeping or hopping from the bottom to the top of a tree requires less energy than flying the same vertical distance. In addition, a bird acquires potential energy when it reaches the tree top, as it can launch itself from the top and partially glide to the bottom of a nearby tree, enjoying something of a "free ride." A bird using the reverse strategy, working from top to bottom, would gain some advantage while proceeding downward but would have to expend a great deal of energy flying up to the top of the next tree. Most crucially, though, the mechanical advantage gained by using both feet and tail to support the body in a head-up, vertical position disappears once the bird starts inching downward tailfirst. The tip of the bird's tail would repeatedly catch in the rough bark and suffer abrasion, and the bird would not be able to see where it was going or where to place its feet for a good grip. Finally, since the objective is to locate and capture prey with its bill, a bird traveling upward has its eyes and weapon in the right place, the front end. The same bird struggling down backward would flush its prey without ever having seen it. The only birds that frequently proceed down a trunk are the nuthatches, which do it perched sideways or even upside down and never use the tail for a prop.

Birds scale a tree trunk by hopping, not walking. The head and upper body duck down toward the tree and forward, bringing the center of gravity closer to the trunk and imparting forward motion. Then both feet are thrust forward simultaneously to a new grip. The result is a hitching movement, inching slowly upward. This technique apparently works poorly in the opposite direction. In a head-down position, only the hind claws support any of the bird's weight. Nuthatches move one leg at a time when moving down a trunk. Tree squirrels, which appear to defy gravity while running down trees, have reversible hind feet that allow their claws always to point upward. Birds have not yet mastered that trick. The brown creeper has strongly curved claws on its front toes, but the hind claw is barely curved at all. Thus the creeper, which uses its tail as a prop while climbing, probably could not climb downward headfirst even if it tried to because its inadequately curved rear claws would not permit a secure grip.

These birds represent independent attempts, by members of three different songbird families, to exploit the tree trunk environment. All use the basic anisodactyl foot—that is, three toes pointed forward and one toe to the rear. They all use long strong toes and curved claws to achieve a firm grip on the tree. The short tails of the nuthatches probably facilitate their acrobatic maneuvers. The tail length of the warbler is typical of the other species in its family. The creeper has lengthened and stiffened its tail to function as a prop. Two other passerine families, woodcreepers and ovenbirds, which live only in tropical America, have also solved the problem. Virtually all the woodcreepers and a few of the ovenbirds climb tree trunks in a similar fashion, using lengthened and stiffened tails as a brace.

Woodpeckers (which are not songbirds) have adapted most successfully to the vertical tree trunk and have done so using a different foot structure. Avian anatomists have assigned numbers to the four digits of the basic avian foot to assist in tracing homologous structures (see Figure 2-1, p. 47). The inner toe, middle toe, and outer toe are designated as II, III, and IV respectively, while the hind toe, or hallux, is number I. (Compare this with your hand, with the opposable digit, your thumb, being I, your index finger II, middle finger III, ring finger IV, and little finger V.) This is the basic anisodactyl (unevenly divided toes) foot, three toes facing forward, one to the rear. Woodpeckers have a zygodactyl (yoke-toed) foot, with the outer toe rotated to the rear. Thus this foot has two toes (II and III) pointing forward and two (I and IV) to the rear. While this arrangement might seem awkward, it makes for an efficient grasping foot well adapted to perching. Parrots, cuckoos, and toucans have this foot as well. This foot can work equally well on land, as it does for the speedy Roadrunner of cartoon fame, who is a caricature of the fleet-footed cursorial cuckoo that inhabits our arid Southwest.

There are some 200 species of woodpeckers in the world, and as one might expect in such a large and successful group, considerable diversity exists in their arboreal adaptations. Some are essentially "ground" woodpeckers, finding most of their food on the ground or in fallen logs. Our northern flicker (which once had two names) is a good example of this group. It was the yellow-shafted flicker in the eastern United States and the red-shafted flicker in the West before taxonomist finally agreed they were merely color variations of the same species. The flicker, in all its colors, forages on ants and termites on the ground or dug out of rotten logs. Two of its toes face forward, joined together along their basal phalanges (the small bones found in fingers and toes) so that they act almost as a single unit. The two toes facing to the rear are not joined together, and toe IV, the outermost, may occasionally rotate to the outside when the bird is perched on a tree trunk. The longest toe is toe III, facing forward.

The arboreal, or tree-dwelling, woodpeckers have followed two different paths in adapting to vertical tree trunks. First, the basal phalanges of the front toes II and III have become relatively short and the toes are able to spread apart and attain a broader grip. The outer fourth toe has become the longest toe and has shifted to the outside so that it now extends nearly perpendicular to the anterior toes. The small hallux, toe I, now has no function. The two anterior toes and the tail support the weight of the bird. The outer fourth toe of each foot provides a pincer grip and counteracts the tendency to fall backward away from the trunk. The hallux, pointing downward, holds nothing. It frequently lies sideways against the trunk with its claw nonfunctional. The downy and hairy woodpeckers, small and medium-size variations of the same body style, have small hallux feet of this nature. The arctic and three-toed woodpeckers of northern North America have gone one step farther. They have lost the halluces completely. Toes II and III point forward, toe IV is held laterally, and the loss of toe I does not seem to have impaired tree-climbing abilities in any way.

Each of the toes has a different number of phalanges. Toe I has two phalanges, just as the human thumb and large toe have. Toe II has three phalanges, as do all other digits in human hands and feet. But birds go us one better, for toes III and IV have four and five phalanges respectively. This makes it easy for us to keep track of which toe is going in which direction on woodpecker feet.

The large pileated woodpecker, which is arboreal, has feet very much like a flicker's. The fourth toe rotates to the outside when the bird perches vertically, and it is shorter than toe III. The hallux still exists and has a large, strong claw, though the toe itself is rather short. Pileated woodpeckers spend a good bit of time drilling into dead tree trunks for carpenter ants and other prey, but they also do the same on fallen logs and on the ground. On the ground the foot assumes a typical zygodactyl position, two toes forward and two to the rear. Thus this species seems to reside halfway between the ground woodpeckers and the arboreal species.

The ivory-billed woodpecker, the largest of our native woodpeckers, now apparently extinct, demonstrated the extreme condition of the second adaptation that enables vertical perching. Both hind toes, I and IV, have rotated to the outer side of the foot. The hallux not only is larger, with a strong claw, but also shifts to the other side of the foot and joins the base of toe IV. The bird can direct all four toes forward when necessary, with toe IV the longest. Observations and photographs of the ivory-billed woodpeckers reveal that they held their legs at an angle to the tree axis and placed the tarsus (the lower leg bone) against or very close to the tree trunk. Other woodpeckers hold their legs beneath their bodies, paralleling the tree axis, and hold their tarsi away from the trunk. The ivory-billeds, by spreading their legs apart at an angle to the trunk axis, were able to achieve a firm grip while bringing their bodies closer to the trunk and allowing a greater length of the tail feathers to contact the trunk, providing greater support.

Thus we see that the more arboreal woodpeckers have converted the zygodactyl foot, which is best suited for perching, into a true scansorial foot, better adapted for climbing, by

FIGURE 2-2 Pileated woodpecker.

rotating the outermost toe, the fourth, to a point where it functions laterally. The hallux may still exist, has shrunk, has disappeared completely, or has shifted to the outside. These are all variations on the same theme. To use clinging to a vertical tree trunk as a major foraging strategy, the bird must develop some means of achieving a lateral pincer grip. Birds, such as the songbirds, that employ the ancestral anisodactyl grip to forage on tree trunks, with a single rear toe opposing three forward toes, do not achieve any substantial body size.

The 21 woodpeckers found north of Mexico range in size from the diminutive downy woodpecker, a mere 5¾ inches long, to the 18-inch ivory-billed woodpecker. One might expect the other species to range widely in size between these two extremes. This is not the case. The pileated woodpecker is 15 inches long, followed by the 10½-inch flicker and the 9-inch Lewis's woodpecker. At the other extreme, the second-smallest species is the 6¾-inch Nuttall's woodpecker. The other 15 species are between 7 and 9 inches in length. Clearly there appears to be an optimum size for woodpeckers, as three-fourths of our species conform to a very narrow range at the smaller end of the scale.

Perching on a tree trunk, rather than a branch, changes the angle of gravitational pull on a bird by ninety degrees. The three major bones of a perching bird leg typically form a Z pattern. Avian leg bones are quite different from those of mammals. In humans, for example, we have a single bone, the femur, which connects to the pelvis and extends to the knee. From there two bones, the tibia and the fibula, extend to the foot. A number of tarsal and metatarsal bones form the foot, the basic walking surface, which ends in five toes. The avian femur is quite similar to a human's. The tibia is the dominant bone below the knee, and the fibula has virtually disappeared. The true avian knee, known to lovers of fried chicken as the joint between the drumstick and thigh, hides from view beneath skin and feathers. The lowermost leg bone, a conglomeration of bones called the tarsometatarsus, is generally

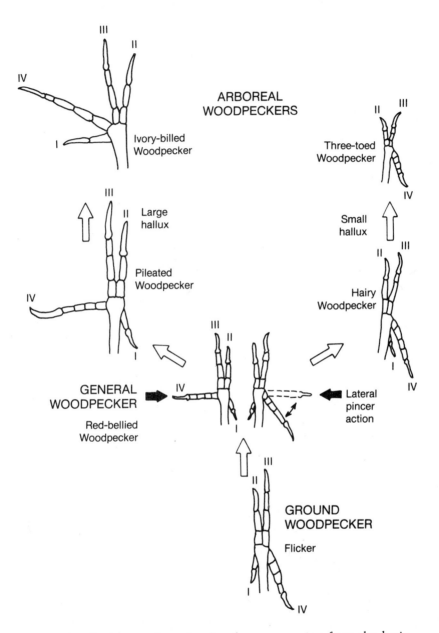

FIGURE 2-3 Evolution of woodpecker feet, progressing from the basic zygodactyl foot of the ground foragers (flicker), to a lateral shift of the 4th digit (red-bellied woodpecker), diverging to two paths, either reduction (hairy woodpecker) and loss (three-toed woodpecker) of the hind toe, or enlargement (pileated woodpecker) and shift to opposite side (ivory-billed woodpecker) of the hind toe in the arboreal foragers.

naked, devoid of muscles or feathers, and seldom makes it as far as the supermarket. The toes attach to the end of this "tarsus," forming the bird's "foot." Humans stand upon feet; birds stand on their toes. What we think of as naked knees when we view a bird are more closely akin to ankles. That explains why the leg appears to bend in the wrong direction. When a human bends a knee to stand on one leg, the foot rises behind the body; when a bird bends its "ankle" to stand similarly, its foot rises in front of the body.

Gravity pulls down and tends to collapse the Z formed by the leg bones of a bird standing on the ground. The leg muscles work to extend and straighten the leg to hold the body up. When the bird rotates 90 degrees to a vertical, head-up position on a tree trunk, the gravity's pull shifts to the rear of the bird. This shift pulls the body away from the tree and forces the legs to straighten, extending away from the tree which the bird is grasping with its claws. Thus the muscular action needed to counteract the pull of gravity is one which flexes (bends) the leg rather than one which extends it. Accordingly, the less important extensor muscles of woodpecker legs are smaller and weaker, while the more developed flexor muscles are larger and stronger than those typical of perching birds.

As the woodpecker's feet and leg muscles adapted to perching on tree trunks, its tail feathers, particularly the central pair, grew longer and stronger. All woodpeckers, except the small primitive piculets of the tropics, use their tails as sturdy props when they are perched on vertical trunk surfaces. Woodpecker tails are typically black or brown, and the melanin pigments deposited during formation of the feathers add greatly to their strength and ability to resist wear and tear. The tail feathers have sturdy shafts and typically come to a point that increases their grip on the tree trunk. The terminal vertebrae, to which the tail feathers and controlling muscles are attached, also increase in size.

The second major adaptation of the woodpecker is its

FIGURE 2-4 Gravitational force (broad arrows) tends to collapse the Z-configuration of the three leg bones in a ground forager, thus major muscular action (narrow arrows) extend the leg; gravity pulls a treetrunk forager backwards, extending the leg bones, thus major muscles fold the leg to hold body close to the treetrunk.

strong bill and woodpecking habit. Again, comparison with tree trunk-foraging songbirds is instructive. The thin bill of the black-and-white warbler is typical of all other warblers, perfect for gleaning insects from leaves and small branches but ill suited for pecking. Likewise, the bill of the brown creeper is thin and slightly downcurved, ideal for extracting prey from narrow bark crevices but useless for excavating. Nuthatches have heavy, strong bills, which they use to open acorns and other nuts they wedge into bark crevices, but they do not excavate wood-boring insects. They eat only prey found on tree trunk surfaces or hidden in crevices.

The length of North American woodpecker bills ranges from less than 1 inch in the smaller species to nearly 3 inches in the largest species, the ivory-billed woodpecker. The size of the bill varies directly with the size of the bird. While the proportional length of the bill can differ slightly compared with the length of the bird or the length of its skull, a longer bill basically reflects a larger body.

Woodpecker bills are either pointed or chisel-shaped at the tip. Both function well for excavation, but the chisel shape, found in the hairy and pileated woodpeckers, for example, seems to facilitate removal of larger wood chunks. While the mere mention of woodpeckers conjures up images of industrious birds vigorously attacking tree trunks, hacking out nest holes or juicy grubs with equal abandon, not all woodpeckers excavate wood-boring insects for food. Woodpecking and drumming require extensive strengthening of the skull and its associated muscles to permit the head and brain of the bird to withstand and absorb the hammering force.

Those woodpeckers that do hammer on trees a great deal also differ from one another in their manner of delivering blows to the tree trunk. The yellow-bellied sapsucker holds its body close to the trunk, with its leg parallel and often in contact with the tree. It delivers blows solely with the neck. The hairy woodpecker also holds its body close to the trunk but adds a little upper body motion to the neck blow. The three-toed woodpecker really gets into hammering. It holds its abdomen away from the trunk, moving its center of gravity farther from the tree. The curve of its neck does not straighten during delivery of the blow. Instead, the body develops momentum as its torso flexes backward preparing to strike and straightens during the forward motion. The entire body whips forward and rotates about the ball-and-socket joint where the femur of the legs joins the pelvis. As the forward motions begins, the heel of the foot and the tarsus lose contact with the trunk so that only the toenails are touching the tree. At the instant of bill contact the tip of the tail may briefly leave the trunk. This action appears to represent the ultimate efficiency in woodpecking technique, and both the three-toed woodpecker and its close relative the black-backed woodpecker specialize in excavating wood borers in the boreal forest.

The tongue of the woodpecker has adapted into a specialized, extensible organ of fantastic dexterity. It can protrude beyond the tip of the bill several inches in some species and terminates in a hard, horny tip armed with minute spines. Once a woodpecker penetrates the tunnel of a wood-boring insect larva, it can explore the tunnel with its tongue, pierce the soft body of the larva with the sharp horny tip, and extract the prey impaled upon the spines. Large salivary glands produce a sticky mucus that lubricates the tongue to allow smooth passage through insect tunnels and snag ants and other insects on the surface of the tongue. Woodpeckers relish ants and termites and seem oblivious of the bites or the formic acid secreted by the ants. Flickers, which generally favor ants, have very few spines on the tips of their tongues. Hairy woodpeckers, which concentrate on extracting wood-boring beetle larvae from their tunnels, have sharply barbed tongues. The tongues of sapsuckers terminate in numerous, very minute spines that are little more than hairs and form a brushy tip that helps them consume liquid sap.

A V-shaped cartilage, called the hyoid, supports the tongue

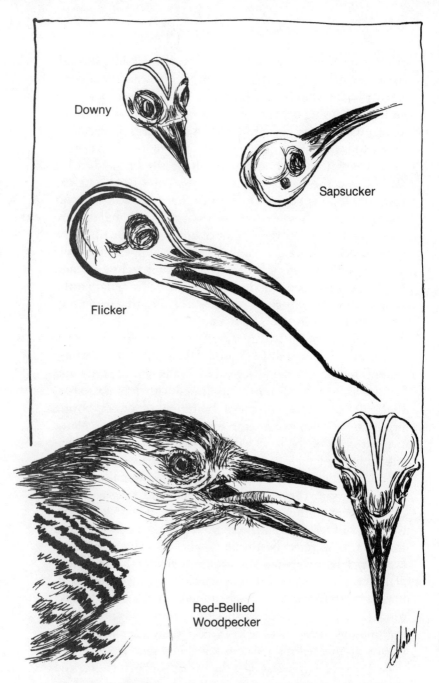

FIGURE 2-5 The hyoid cartilages of the sapsucker barely reach the top of its head, while those of the downy and red-bellied woodpeckers extend forward and reach the eyes. The flicker is extreme in that its hyoids pass through the nostril into the upper bill.

of the woodpecker. The arms, or horns, of the cartilage extend from the base of the tongue past the hinges of the lower jaw, around each side of the neck and up to the rear of the skull, where they curve up the back of the head and unite on top of the head. In those species, such as the sapsuckers, whose tongues do not extend far, the hyoid horns stop between the eyes on top of the head. In other species, such as the red-bellied woodpecker, the hyoid horns continue forward side by side until they reach the base of the bill. In the flicker, a ground forager that specializes in raiding anthills, the hyoid horns continue forward through the bony structure and beyond the nasal chambers to near the tip of the bill. Thus in this species, with an extremely far-reaching tongue that can explore the depths of anthill chambers, the hyoid horns start in the tongue, circle beneath, around, and on top of the skull, to terminate in the bill lying above their starting place in the tongue.

Subtleties in anatomical structure are reflected in behavioral changes as well. The downy and hairy woodpeckers are near look-alikes and live throughout North America. They appear to be small and medium-size versions of the same basic "woodpecker design." Downy woodpeckers forage in small trees and shrubs, as well as in large trees, and frequent the very tips of branches, often hanging upside down. They tap and peck for prey but rarely excavate deeply. The tongue of a downy woodpecker extends a bare 7 mm beyond its 16 mm bill, and its hyoid horns stop on the top of the head above the eyes. The hairy woodpecker forages on tree trunks and larger branches and, unlike the downy woodpecker, will spend considerable time digging out a deep wood borer. Its hyoid horns circle over the head, pass into the bony orbit that protects the eyes, and coil around inside the orbit behind the eyeball. When the long, slender muscle that parallels each horn for its entire length contracts, the horns are pulled forward and the tongue extends a considerable distance beyond the tip of the bill.

Woodpeckers are typically black and white, be it in spots, large patches, or zebra stripes, enlivened with a bold splash of red. In some, like the red-headed woodpecker, the entire head and neck of both sexes are bright red. In many species the amount of red on the head serves to distinguish the sexes. The ivory-billed woodpecker, for example, has a large, erect crest of feathers. The posterior half of the crest is bright red in the male but entirely black in the female. The large male pileated woodpecker has a large red crest and a red mustache while the female has less red on the crown and a black mustache. In most species the female has either no red on the head or less red than the male. Immature males usually lack the red head pattern, and it is generally believed this absence of red quells any aggressiveness the adult male might show toward its male offspring. The red-cockaded woodpecker is a bit unusual in its coloration. Adults have a very similar appearance. The male has a tiny area of red at the top of the white side of his head, a red "cockade" visible only when consciously erected during territorial defense or sexual displays. Yet the entire center of the crown of an immature male is red. In this instance the presence of a red crown defuses male aggression. The young of downy and hairy woodpeckers, close relatives of the red-cockaded, share this red-headed characteristic.

Woodpeckers communicate frequently, through distinctive vocalizations and drumming. Bird watchers typically first locate woodpeckers by the sounds they make: calls, tapping, percussions, and the noise of falling debris. Most woodpeckers have a large repertoire of calls that serve to proclaim territories, maintain contact between individual birds, and sound the alarm at the approach of predators. Unique to woodpeckers is communication by drumming. Drumming involves rapid percussion on a resonating surface, such as a dead limb or sturdy utility pole, or, in urban areas, a metal gutter spout or garbage can. The resulting sound carries long distances and indicates to virtually everyone within earshot the presence of a woodpecker. Its principal function seems to be to attract a mate and to declare and maintain an established territory.

Thus we have learned how woodpeckers differ from other birds in the way adaptations in their legs, feet, and tails permit them to perch and move about on vertical trunk surfaces. They also have evolved a number of adaptations in the structure of the head, bill, and tongue that allow them to hammer upon and dig into the limbs and trunks of trees to obtain food, excavate nesting and roosting cavities, and communicate. It is interesting to speculate on which of these adaptive complexes arose first. Did the possession of strong bill capable of excavating wood-boring insects lead the woodpecker to modify natural tree cavities and finally create entirely new cavities? Were woodpeckers capable of excavation before the development of a unique foot that permitted stable perching on vertical trunks?

Comparison with their closest relatives may shed some light on these questions. There are five other families of birds in addition to the woodpecker family in the avian order Piciformes. All these families have zygodactyl feet, but none has developed a climbing foot similar to that of the woodpeckers. The largest family is the barbets of Asia, Africa, and the New World tropics, which have short but large and heavy bills and feed on fruits and insects. They typically perch quietly and sally forth to capture insects in flight, and they nest in holes which they dig in earthen banks or excavate in well-rotted trees.

The puffbirds of the Neotropics have large, strong bills and feed principally on insects which they capture using perch-and-sally flycatching techniques. Puffbirds nest in holes in banks or in tunnels on level ground, which they dig with their bills and feet. Some species excavate holes in the sides of arboreal termite nests. The New World jacamars have long, straight bills, with which they capture large insects, particularly butterflies and dragonflies, using perch-and-sally methods. Jacamars also nest in holes in banks.

The Neotropical toucans have exceptionally large but very lightweight bills that function well in gathering fruits, large insects, nestling birds, and lizards but are useless for excavating nest cavities. Toucans nest in natural tree cavities or cavities excavated by other species. The Old World honeyguides have relatively small bills and feed on insects, especially bees and wasps. Honeyguides are nest parasites that lay their eggs in the nests of other species and build no nests of their own at all.

Barbets, puffbirds, jacamars, toucans, and honeyguides do not forage on tree trunks, and all lack the specialized foot necessary to perch on vertical surfaces. Some of these birds nest in natural cavities, but few excavate their own cavities in trees. None of these birds feed on wood-boring insects.

When we examine the woodpeckers of the world, we find a few ground woodpeckers that excavate tunnels in banks for nesting, as our own flicker occasionally does in the treeless southwestern United States. One flicker found in the Andes of South America even nests in closely spaced colonies, indicating a scarcity of suitable nesting banks. We also find a number of woodpeckers that spend a great deal of time foraging for insects, using the perch-and-sally flycatching technique. Many woodpeckers, particularly those species with a less specialized foot, also consume quantities of fruits and nuts.

It thus appears that hole-nesting relatives of woodpeckers are quite common, and a broad variety of bill types can be used to excavate cavities in earth or rotten trees. So cavity excavation probably antedates foraging on tree trunks. Also, a number of woodpeckers have specialized woodpecking capabilities but use this tool to excavate cavities, open nut hulls, and store nuts in tree bark crevices without fulfilling the final step of excavating wood-boring larvae. It seems clear that the ability to peck wood evolved before the ability to forage efficiently on vertical tree trunks.

It is also clear that bark foraging on tree trunks is a unique way of life mastered by very few birds. None of the woodpecker relatives is a bark forager. Only a handful of the abundant songbirds, which seem to exploit every way of life imaginable, have mastered the technique of clinging to a vertical tree trunk. A well-stocked food pantry, rarely raided by other birds, is available to woodpeckers.

Ornithologists have long known the answer to that ageless question "Which came first, the chicken or the egg?" Our reptilian ancestors first developed the shelled egg, long before the first chick ever pipped its eggshell and emerged into the real world. Likewise, the first woodpeckers were most likely depositing their eggs in tree cavities of their own making long before they were able to cling to vertical tree trunks and exploit a new food resource, the creatures that live in bark crevices and the tunneling larvae of wood-boring insects.

Some birds are known to have their population size limited by the number of available nest sites. If they cannot obtain a suitable natural cavity in a relatively safe location, they are less able to raise offspring successfully. When artificial cavities are provided by humans, the population may increase, demonstrating that food and other resources have not been limiting factors. When humans remove dead trees from a forest, the number of available nest sites for woodpeckers and other hole nesters is reduced and populations decline. Foresters and wildlife managers have belatedly recognized that dead trees are a critical resource for hole-nesting birds and other animals.

Perhaps the ability to excavate their own cavities as needed has led to the success that woodpeckers have enjoyed around the world. The red-cockaded woodpecker is a small arboreal species with a small hallux that has extended this capability one more step: It can excavate a cavity in a living tree. This unique capability will be explored further in Chapter Four, but let us first examine the causes of extinction.

CHAPTER THREE

Extinction Is Forever

LIFE BEGAN, PERHAPS once or twice, three billion or so years ago, under earthly conditions which no longer exist. Since that moment the thread of life has continued unbroken to this day as the earliest organisms, and the most recent, have repeatedly responded to their changing environment and evolved into new and better adapted forms. The overwhelming diversity of past and present creatures is vivid testimony to the efficacy of this evolutionary process. But environmental change is constant, and those organisms that were unable to cope with new environmental demands perished. A few were fossilized and became inert testimony to past evolution, providing tantalizing clues to our origins and forebears.

56

Extinction is as old as life itself and as natural as death, for it is merely the death of all individuals of a given species. Each species represents a unique combination of genetic material, or genome, honed and pruned for thousands of years by environmental influences and mutational chance. This genome, once lost, can never surface again in the evolutionary process, for no population will ever experience an identical environmental or mutational history. Once a species slips over the brink of extinction, its genetic heritage disappears forever.

How do species go extinct? Through very simple arithmetic. If the number of individuals born does not equal or exceed the number that dies, the population will dwindle and eventually vanish. The time frame necessary for extinction to occur varies considerably. Extinction can be a protracted process, barely perceptible as populations wax and wane from year to year, tracking climatic variables or other subtle influences, or it can be episodic, produced by a single catastrophe acting upon a small local population, all members of which perish simultaneously from the same fatal cause. More typically, extinction takes place over several generations or more of the organism.

Why do species go extinct? The number of specific reasons may be nearly equal the number of extinct species. But we can generalize to some extent and state that the causes of extinction fall into four categories.

One major cause is widespread environmental change, especially change that makes life impossible in a given habitat. Organisms living in our oceans, lakes, and streams seem to be more susceptible to such threats. Land-dwelling organisms are bathed in air, which dissolves nothing and supports very little. Water, the world's greatest solvent, surrounds aquatic organisms from birth to death. Pollutants, be they natural or artifacts of man, dissolve to varying degrees in this great solvent medium. Thus aquatic organisms are swimming in pollutants, from which there is no escape. We see this pollution at work today in the form of acid precipitation, as rain or dry particles. The combustion of fossil fuels (made from the bodies of extinct organisms) spews chemicals into the atmosphere as pollutants, the result of man's ever-increasing appetite for energy. These pollutants, in the form of gases and solid particles, travel through the atmosphere and undergo transformations en route to other chemical forms. Since the law of gravity has not yet been repealed, everything that goes up must eventually come down someplace. This someplace must be either a body of water or the watershed that eventually leads to a body of water. There are very few other places to go. Sooner or later, riding on raindrops and rivulets, these pollutants end up in an aquatic ecosystem.

Some pollutants increase the acidity of a body of water. Such an increase in acidity endangers the inhabitants of that body of water, particularly fish, and can kill them off in a variety of ways. High acidity can directly cause the death of adult and juvenile fish, for example, in vivid style, with dead and dying fish floating on the surface of the water. It can also lead to the deaths of other organisms important in the food chain leading to the fish, so that the fish die more slowly of starvation or become weakened and succumb to disease or predation. Perhaps the larger fish do not die from the toxic environment, but their eggs and offspring do not survive. This form of death takes longer as the adult and juvenile fish may live out their life-spans but new young do not replenish the population. In one generation all the fish will be gone. Should the acidic waters poison all the populations of a given species, that species will eventually become extinct. Acid rain is currently toxifying many North American and European lakes and killing off their fish and other aquatic organisms. If acid rain keeps spreading geographically, as appears likely, the extinction of some species is inevitable.

Land ecosystems seem more resistant to environmental change because they are inherently more "open," with numerous connections to surrounding areas. This openness allows animals to move away from incompatible environmental conditions. Should an environmental change be widespread, however, no alternative habitat may be available. Slow change, such as the march of glaciers over parts of the Northern Hemisphere, might permit organisms to stay ahead of the change and locate refuge areas. Large-scale deforestation, now rampant in the tropics, is wreaking havoc as it destroys the habitat of less mobile animals that lack any other suitable habitat to invade. Many tropical birds, including woodpeckers, are likely to succumb to this devastation of their forest habitat.

A second cause of extinction is the loss of a natural resource. Obviously related to the environmental change we just considered, the loss of a natural resource connotes the disappearance of a particular component of the environment. The habitat itself may not appear to have changed, but a component vital to some species may decline or disappear, drastically affecting species dependent upon that component. An example of a lost resource might be the disappearance of a food source or prey species. Most animals have a moderately broad diet and do not depend upon a single species of plant or animal for sustenance. If one food item declines or disappears, they can shift and adapt to alternative sources. Any species that is totally dependent upon only one or two food items will flirt with extinction if the food item itself becomes extinct.

Study of the snail or everglade kite has shown us how tenuous the survival of a food specialist can be. This hawk feeds almost exclusively on apple snails that inhabit freshwater marshes in the lowland tropics of the Americas. The kite's bill is long, thin, and sharply downcurved—ideal for extracting snails, of a particular size, from their spiral shells. This kite inhabits a broad geographical range, from Mexico to Argentina and Uruguay, with isolated populations in Florida and Cuba. By depending entirely on snails for food (an unusual prey in the world of raptors), the kite has linked its fate inexorably to that of the apple snail, which in turn depends on the health and persistence of freshwater marshes. Florida once provided a home for a sizable, but perhaps never truly abundant, kite population. Now, however, Florida marshlands have shrunk because of draining for agriculture or mosquito control, and excessive human consumption and pollution have lowered and degraded the water table. As the quantity of marshlands has declined, the snail populations have shrunk, and the number of snail kites has dropped precipitously, to fewer than one hundred.

Resources used in reproduction are also critical. Microhabitats such as grass beds, gravel bars, isolated islands, or beaches may be critical to successful reproduction. Woodpeckers, for example, typically require dead trees or branches for nest cavities. When foresters started removing dead trees, or "snags" in the jargon of foresters, from forests to prevent the spread of disease (or so they thought they were doing), nest sites became very scarce and woodpecker populations declined. A major research effort demonstrated the value of snags to woodpeckers, and of woodpeckers to the forests and foresters, and reversed management policy in order to promote retention of dead trees in our woodlands.

As natural resources essential for daily maintenance or reproduction become scarce, competition for the available resources increases and creates a third cause of extinction. The "struggle for survival" between competing species has been a cornerstone of evolutionary and ecological thought for decades. However, as we shall explore in detail later, competition is philosophically alluring but frequently hard to demonstrate in the real world. Theoretically, if two species are competing for an identical resource of limited supply, only one of the species will eventually survive. It is easy to conjure up instances when competing species have altered slightly their physical requirements to facilitate mutual survival. Since they have been working at this coexistence for thousands of years, it is frequently difficult to demonstrate that they were direct competitors a few millennia ago.

The final cause of extinction is perhaps the easiest to envision: organisms, whether predator, parasite, or pathogen, that cause a direct loss of life. We can point to countless historical examples of predators, especially man himself, that directly contribute to the demise of various species. In fact, predators themselves are frequently the first animals to become extinct at the hands of man. Few voices rose to stop the local extinction of wolves, mountain lions, and bears from the eastern states as colonists invaded North America. So, too, went the edible species, the wood buffalo, deer, and turkey, without a cry. Even today hunters who would be proud to "get the last one" stalk the forests each fall. The efficacy of predators in exterminating prey further appears in the success of those preservation programs that stopped the hunting of near-extinct species and allowed them to recover to some semblance of their former abundance.

Which of these four categories best explains the problems of the red-cockaded and ivory-billed woodpeckers? Well, we cannot absolutely ignore any one. A climatic change would be readily detectable and affect many other species in the southeastern forests. This does not appear to be the case. However, environmental change must also include the widespread application of pesticides and the subsequent contamination of the environment. Several species, such as the peregrine falcon, bald eagle, and brown pelican, have been at the brink of extinction because of toxic pesticides. These species were all top predators at the end of aquatic food chains that accumulated pesticides at each transfer point between prey and predator. Our woodpeckers operate at lower levels of consumption, and humans have not spread pesticides widely in the forests the birds inhabit. Both the red-cockaded and the ivory-billed woodpeckers originally lived in the area from Texas to the East Coast, and their demise has not been a local phenomenon. So environmental change has probably not been a major exterminating factor.

Loss of a natural resource is a prime candidate for the de-

cline of both species. The loss of large, old riverbottom hardwood trees appears to have crippled the ivory-billed woodpecker, and the loss of large, mature pine trees has similarly
affected the red-cockaded woodpecker. Both instances involve a general loss of habitat, as riverbottom forests have
given way to agriculture and pine forests have fallen under the
clearcutting blade of pine plantations. We will consider these
trends in more detail later.

Competition cannot be ignored in this analysis. The southeastern woodpecker guild includes nine species. All of these
evolved together in apparent harmony, neatly parceling the
available resources among themselves, as we shall learn. Yet if
habitat loss has been widespread, as it appears to have been,
these species may have crowded one another into more competitive ecological niches. We will try later to define the roles
which these nine species appear to play in our ecological thea-
ter.

Predation will prove less tractable to analysis. We know
that hawks, and most likely owls, too, prey upon red-cockaded woodpeckers. We note the cautionary behavior and
alarm calls of woodpeckers when hawks are nearby. But
hawks in these forests tend to be generalists, hunting prey of
appropriate size wherever they can find it and capture it. No
hawk appears to specialize in woodpeckers, and certainly the
rarity of red-cockadeds would lead to slim pickings for a predator (a certain amount of circular reasoning is involved here,
because we cannot prove that intensive predation did not
lead to their present scarcity). However, the woodpeckers and
hawks have coexisted for a long time, and no evidence suggests that hawks are putting undue pressure on woodpecker
populations. Although woodpeckers may occasionally succumb to a bored or youthful human hunter, they are not
desirable game species, and hunting has not played a role in
their decline.

Certain tree-climbing snakes are also predators of woodpecker eggs and nestlings. That they can be significant preda-

tors appears in the development of an antisnake defense strategy by red-cockaded woodpeckers, which we shall explore in greater depth in Chapter Four. But snakes as hunters are generalists, rather than specialists, consuming the eggs and nestlings of any birds they may encounter. Snake populations do not seem to have increased. If they had, other bird species, particularly hole nesters, should also be disappearing in the face of increased predation, but there is no evidence of this. Predation seems to play only a minor role in our ecological drama.

Pathogens and parasites constitute a problem for our analysis of shrinking woodpecker populations. To gather direct evidence would involve sacrificing already rare birds for autopsy. So we must settle for indirect evidence. Researchers have captured and handled a relatively large number of red-cockaded woodpeckers over the past two decades. They have placed various combinations of colored plastic bands on their legs so that they can recognize and identify specific individuals as they go about their daily habits. Had any substantial number of these birds been diseased, the researchers would have noticed the symptoms of emaciation and poor feather condition. Since investigators have not noticed these conditions, we can assume that pathogens and parasites have not contributed to the demise of the woodpeckers.

Species go extinct one individual at a time. What are the causes of death? The most obvious causes are biological, and foremost among them must be lack of food. An individual must find enough food containing all the essential chemicals for continuance of life or it shall cease to exist. Actually the individual must find more than enough food during certain times of the year to ensure that the species persists. Reproduction demands energy and nutrients beyond subsistence levels. Finding a suitable mate and courtship consume energy. Defending a territory from competitors for resources takes energy. The production of one or more eggs is perhaps the greatest drain on energy and nutrients in the life of many female organisms. Without good nutrition a female can produce no eggs or too few eggs to offset natural losses. Without a surplus of food the adults cannot properly incubate their eggs and simultaneously maintain their own nutritional needs. Without a surplus of food in the immediate vicinity of the nest the adults cannot feed the voracious hatchlings. Once the hatchlings fledge and can accompany the parents farther afield to feed, the food supply must be capable of supporting a sudden tripling of the population, as two adults plus four offspring would represent. Even while gaining independence, inexperienced young require surplus food to offset their ineptitude in acquiring it. Young birds are slow to develop expertise in capturing prey species that flee in defense or in locating camouflaged prey that freeze and "disappear" from view. Clearly, abundant food is critical to successful reproduction.

From the instant of conception a new individual is prey: while still within the female's body, if she is captured; as a silent and immobile egg in a nest; as a perhaps noisy but equally defenseless nestling; and as an inexperienced juvenile learning to recognize real world dangers. For woodpeckers, predators can appear as snakes, hawks, owls, even humans. While predators usually take the form of animals large enough to capture and consume their prey, much smaller parasites and pathogens can be no less dangerous. In these instances a few "predators" may not be lethal, but too many can overwhelm the defenses of the animal and lead to death. Some nest parasites are quite capable of remaining inert in a nesting cavity until a year has passed and a new crop of "prey" appears in the nest. Woodpeckers probably construct a new nesting cavity each year as much to elude the parasites' attacks as for any other reason. Red-cockaded woodpeckers inhabit their cavities year-round but ideally have more than one cavity per bird available, and they frequently switch between them.

Accidental injury is the final biological cause of death. Narrow escapes from predators can result in infections or crip-

pled animals that are more vulnerable to subsequent predators. Animals typically settle territorial disputes without injury to either party. Clashes with larger species attempting to
evict a cavity owner may be more damaging. Larger woodpeckers sometimes injure smaller ones while physically eject-
ing them from cavities. The loss of life to predators, parasites,
and competitors seems unlikely to drive woodpeckers to extinction.

Weather, in the form of occasional and chance events or
long-term climatic changes, can also cause death. Woodpeckers retreat to their cavities for protection during severe
weather. Should a cavity tree fall during a thunderstorm, tornado, or hurricane, the occupant may be killed or injured
during the crash. Lightning strikes are especially lethal. Although the tree may survive with little more than a vivid scar
coursing down the trunk, the lightning is likely to electrocute
a woodpecker within a cavity. Direct lightning strikes that kill
a tree outright would seem certain to kill its occupants as well.

Anomalous winter weather that prevents woodpeckers
from foraging for an extended period could lead to starvation
or, at least, a weakened condition that indirectly contributes
to death from some other cause. Climatic changes might have
widespread effects on habitat and prey species, leading to a
scarcity of resources and increased competition sufficient to
push a precariously balanced species over the brink.

Thus death faces individual organisms at every turn and
limits average lifetimes to months, at best a few years. Species
have greater longevity, most usefully measured in millennia,
but seldom with accuracy. Both are natural, predictable
events. If this is the case, why should we be so concerned
about the pending extinction of a handful of species?

We can plead compassion, that we should cherish and protect our fellow passengers on Spaceship Earth, for we may be
the sole inhabitants of the universe. We can invoke religion,
that we have no right to cast aside what God hath placed
upon the earth. Of course, we subvert both these arguments

by the religious zeal we invest in exterminating "pests" from our houses and "weeds" from our lawns and by our world-wide campaigns to eradicate pathogens and their vectors.

We can attribute aesthetic value to our woodland companions and cry out, "Woodman, spare that tree, and the feathered sprite within," but our plea will likely drown in the drone of a chain saw while the woodcutter envisions dollar signs. We can cite the intrinsic interest which wild animals provide and how much they can teach us. While the legion of bird watchers grows each year, they are still considered a fringe element by the bulk of the populace, a little crazy, perhaps, but basically harmless, for they seldom shoot one another.

We can turn to economic values to make our case, citing direct benefits to humanity. Here we may spark more interest and gain a partial hearing, but the going is tough in the capitalistic trenches. The purchase of binoculars and field guides does not generate as many designated tax dollars as the sale of fishing tackle and shotgun shells. Nonconsumptive bird watchers have no need for "open" seasons regulated by a fish and game commission. Practitioners of "take only photographs, leave only footprints" philosophy do not pass through the turnstiles of big-game check-out stations. The ecstatic birder who has just added a new species to his life list has no trophy buck to display on his fender.

We can, with diligent and well-designed study, demonstrate that some woodpeckers remove a certain percentage of bark-boring beetle larvae (or another specific pest) overwintering on commercially valuable trees. We can extrapolate from these results to demonstrate that such bird feeding can prevent insect pest outbreaks from occurring. Insect pests typically reproduce at mind-boggling rates, cycling through a number of generations within a single year. Birds are no match for insects reproductively, being limited to one or two clutches of eggs per year, with no second generation for one or two more years. Insects produce eggs by the hundreds or thousands while for birds, a half dozen eggs would be a phenomenal achievement. So when reproductive conditions are ideal for insects, they are capable of instant response and their populations can experience phenomenal growth. Under these circumstances no predator can keep pace or stand any chance of controlling their population growth. However, these ideal conditions occur infrequently. In the interim, the steady pressures on population growth which woodpeckers, and other birds, are able to exert can, in fact, keep insect populations relatively low. One bird, consuming a hundred or more beetle larvae per day, represents effective pest control over a season or year. If we calculate the number of insects birds eat and the amount of money it would cost to achieve the same degree of control by chemical means, we can estimate the monetary worth of each bird. Unfortunately nobody has made such a calculation for woodpeckers. Studies of this nature are expensive, and more pressing research needs typically beat out woodpeckers, and woodpecker researchers, for available funding resources. It is difficult to prove, though easy to surmise, that woodpeckers habitually prevent insect pest outbreaks from happening.

One study of evening grosbeaks has demonstrated the usefulness of such economic comparisons, however. These finches are a highly mobile, social species with erratic breeding behavior. Flocks of grosbeaks roam widely over our northern states and the Canadian provinces, searching for outbreaks of spruce budworms or other forest insects. When they locate an ample food supply, the grosbeaks quickly reproduce and raise their young on the budworm larvae. This study demonstrated that the annual cost to achieve equivalent insect control through the use of chemical insecticides would be at least $4,700 per square mile of forest treated. Numbers of this magnitude can quickly gain the attention of forest managers and policy makers. We badly need more estimates of how much woodpecker control of forest insect populations is worth in cash terms. However, even if such estimates were available, it would be difficult to rationalize the preservation of an endangered species for its economic contribution to the forest ecosystem alone. By definition, there simply aren't enough red-cockaded and ivory-billed woodpeckers left to register a significant economic contribution. But perhaps if we can preserve the ecosystem for the benefit of the more abundant woodpeckers, we can save the remaining endangered birds in the bargain.

We must turn finally to the structure and function of forest ecosystems to find convincing reasons to preserve endangered species. Life and the universe are hierarchical. Subatomic particles form distinct atoms; atoms form molecules; molecules unite to create macromolecules, many of which are vital to life. Molecules and macromolecules form subcellular structures, which jointly form cells, which have distinct boundaries. Similar cells unite to form tissues; different tissues conjunctively create organs; complementary organs form organ systems, which together create an individual organism, again a distinct, bounded unit. Organisms multiply to form populations, and populations of different species living in contact with one another create communities. Adding in the physical components of the environment transforms communities into ecosystems. The sum of similar and adjacent ecosystems extending over a broad geographical area forms a biome, and the biomes and oceans jointly create the biosphere, once again a distinct, bounded unit. To date we have no confirmation that living organisms extend beyond the exceedingly thin and fragile biosphere on the planet Earth.

We have four discrete units—atoms, cells, organisms, and the biosphere—linked together hierarchically by forms with less distinct boundaries. Yet all must function jointly for life as we know it to persist. The complexity of living organisms is overwhelming. We have seen neither the limits of the universe nor the ultimate subatomic particle. We have barely begun to decipher the intricacies of life. The farther we search, the more we find. But all these parts work together. None can be discarded.

If the boundary of a living organism ruptures, the organism will die unless it can quickly repair the rupture. Should all individuals of a species die, the species itself also dies. This is fortunately less common, because individuals vary greatly and are not equally vulnerable to a given danger. Species are sometimes even hard to define, for they represent one of the great self-deceptions practiced by scientists. Species are defined by their reproductive isolation; for the most part, if two similar organisms are capable of sexually reproducing, they are considered members of the same species. If they are similar in appearance but cannot reproduce, we consider them to have sufficient genetic isolation to be separate species. Yet we frequently name and classify species in total ignorance their reproductive compatibility, and the determination of species distinctions most often depends on the sum of their physical characteristics. I have always admired the honest biologist who stated that "species are what a good taxonomist says they are"; there was a man who knew how to label a spade.

Populations of different species interact with one another, to greater or lesser degrees, to form communities. Some are linked together in food webs. Others merely exploit the same resources. A few do little but share the same living space. Yet each species contributes to a functional role in the ecosystem. Some are key species. For example, if a disease were to wipe out most of the pine trees in a pine forest, the consequences would cascade in all directions as the food sources, shelter habitat, reproductive sites, and so forth disappeared and the effects rippled through all of the dependent species. The ecosystem would totally disintegrate. People achieve this same end when they remove the pine forest using a harvest technique known as clearcutting. They fell the trees and take all the usable logs away. They push the remnants, known as slash, into windrows and subsequently burn them to make way for the planting, many months later, of new pine seedlings. Clearcutting completely disrupts the pine ecosystem, dispersing all the forest inhabitants, and although we plant new pine trees, it will be decades before a mature pine forest will exist on that site again.

Pines are the key species in this mature ecosystem. Other species are less vital. Each has its own place in the structure and functioning of the ecosystem, but their disappearance may not be catastrophic. It may even be hard to predict what, if anything, will happen to the ecosystem in their absence. Neighboring species may adjust to compensate partially for their absence, exploiting the lessened competition for a mutual resource. Predators may shift to alternative prey, increasing pressure on the new victims. If alternative prey is not available, the predator may not reproduce at its previous rate and its population may begin to decline. Everything in an ecosystem is connected to everything else.

In essence the loss of an ecosystem component species is analogous to tinkering with the system. You may remove a part and find that nothing happens, or least it may not be immediately detectable. Or you may remove a part and the whole system collapses. Species have always been removed from ecosystems by extinction. They went extinct long before man set foot on this earth, and they will continue to do so long after he is gone, provided he doesn't manage to take all of them with him in a nuclear holocaust. What has changed is the rate at which species are going extinct. Humans have become an agent of change equal in force to geological phenomena; we have greatly accelerated the pace of extinction. We are playing a dangerous game. Causing the rapid extinction of numerous species is akin to tinkering and throwing away the parts as you take them off. That violates the First

FIGURE 3-1 The web of extinction. The major extinction pressures on red-cockaded woodpeckers typically exert their effects at different trophic levels.

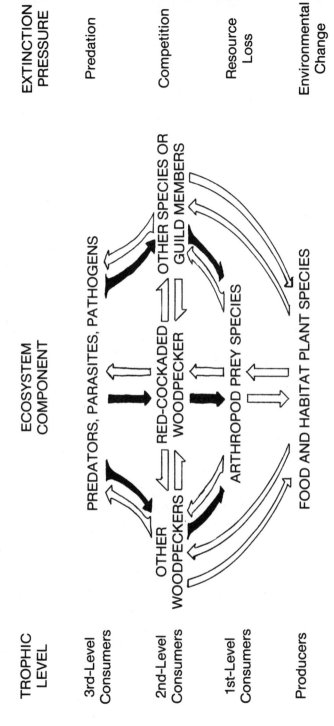

FIGURE 3–1

Law of Tinkering: Never throw away the parts! Once a species goes extinct, that genome is lost forever, and that part of the ecosystem can never be replaced. If you discover that particular part happens to be a vital component, there is no way to obtain a replacement.

The red-cockaded woodpecker lives within an environmental matrix, as depicted in the accompanying figure, a web of extinction. No component exists independent of the others. The four causes of extinction exert their influence differentially on the various components. Various plant species provide food and habitat for arthropods and other consumers. These species, in turn, influence the plant community by means of their plant consumption and role in seed dispersal. The success of the various arthropods affects the number and kinds of secondary consumers that the ecosystem can support. Predation by the secondary consumers correspondingly influences the arthropod community. Direct competition for food and other resources may exist between the secondary consumers. Tertiary predators, parasites, and pathogens affect all of them.

To decipher the role which the red-cockaded and ivory-billed woodpeckers play in the southern forest ecosystems, we have to examine how each fits into the assemblage of nine woodpeckers that inhabit this region and how woodpeckers interact with plants and the other animals in the forests. What essential resources are needed by these endangered species? What impact has human activities had on these resources? What services do woodpeckers provide to the ecosystems? What factors are critical to the successful persistence of these birds?

There Is No Place like This Home

EIGHTY-FIVE SPECIES of birds nest in tree cavities in the forests of North America. They range in size from tiny nuthatches and chickadees to large ducks, mergansers, owls, vultures, and woodpeckers. Many of these birds must depend on decay, disease, or injury to form a natural cavity in a tree. Some must take the cavity just as they find it, able only to do some light housekeeping and perhaps add suitable lining material. If the interior wood has decayed to the point of becoming soft and friable, a few species can enlarge the entrance or the interior to provide a more suitable chamber. The home-making ability of woodpeckers is rare in the bird world.

Having evolved a marvelous tool, its beak, suited to the

excavation of wood- and bark-boring beetles and other arthropods, the woodpecker needs not rely on locating a natural crevice or cavity. It needs only to select a suitable site on a
limb or tree trunk and carve out a customized cavity of its
own, with a perfectly sized entrance hole and interior chamber. Woodpeckers do, in fact, provide many of the cavities
used by other species. Cavities are such a scarce resource that
animals compete intensely for those which do exist. Chickadees and nuthatches can excavate their own cavities in soft
wood if they have to, although they also use natural cavities
or abandoned woodpecker holes when available. But only
woodpeckers consistently create their own cavities or confis-
cate and modify chambers excavated by other, usually smaller
woodpeckers.

Cavity nesting has several advantages over branch nesting.
A small cavity entrance is far less conspicuous than a bulky
twig nest, meaning that predators, always alert for a meal of
eggs or nestlings, are less likely to discover the nest site. Being
nestled in the gloom of a dimly lit chamber has also permitted
cavity nesters to forgo the streaks and speckles on the egg
surface which so effectively camouflage the eggs of ground,
bush, and tree nesters. Woodpecker eggs are uniformly white
and even glossy. Cavities are also easier to defend should a
predator attempt entry while the inhabitant is within. An
incubating woodpecker, armed with a sharp stiletto bill and
powerful neck muscles, defending a narrow entrance hole, is a
formidable opponent to any rat snake searching for an easy
meal. This is one reason cavity nesters typically fledge a
greater percentage of their young than species that use open
nests.

Cavities also provide protection from inclement weather.
The interior will remain dry until wind-driven rain penetrates
the small entrance hole. Wood is a highly efficient insulator,
which tempers both hot and cold temperature extremes. In
hot weather the tree trunk and shaded cavity will be slow to
warm up as direct sunlight strikes the exterior bark. At night

or during cold weather the body heat of the birds remains within the cavity, protecting the occupant from the wind and the debilitating wind chill factor. This same insulating ability of wood can also make warm nights uncomfortable, prompting the occupant to sleep outside, perched on the trunk beneath an overhead limb, benefiting from cool breezes and enjoying the best of both worlds.

The advantages of cavity dwelling extend beyond the nesting season. Many species utilize cavities as year-round shelters in which they place their eggs at the proper season. Each bird will have one or more shelters available to it, sometimes in the same tree, at other times with some distance between them. A bird can use its several cavities to evade a pursuing predator or gain refuge from an impending storm. Nest cavities may subsequently serve as roost cavities at other times of the year. Many species excavate new cavities each year to use as their nest sites.

Most woodpeckers excavate their cavities in dead trees or the dead limbs of living trees because decayed wood is softer and easier to work with. The wood cannot be too soft, though, or it will offer little protection from predators, such as raccoons, that can enlarge the opening to reach the inhabitants. Males do most of the excavation, although females are equally capable. The pace of the work can vary greatly. Excavations begun early in the nesting season may be almost leisurely. Cavities constructed before they are needed for nesting are more prone to usurpation by competing species. Since a cavity generally takes six to ten days to complete, it is often prudent for woodpeckers to excavate just before the nest is needed and to commence egg laying and incubation immediately, assuring full-time occupation of the cavity. It is far easier to defend a cavity against usurpation from within than to attempt to evict an interloper. In addition, when a larger woodpecker species usurps a cavity, it immediately enlarges the opening to facilitate access. This enlarging generally destroys the usefulness of the cavity to its original owner, who subsequently abandons efforts to reclaim it. When displaced in this manner and pressed by the need to lay eggs quickly, the smaller woodpeckers can initiate and complete a new cavity in as few as three days.

A few species can successfully complete cavities in living trees if their interior heartwood has been weakened by fungal infections, a condition known as heartrot. Penetration of the firm trunk perimeter is slow, but once the excavating bird reaches the soft interior, it can quickly complete the chamber. The red-cockaded woodpeckers are unique in their method of cavity construction. They virtually always build in live pine trees. Cavities constructed in dead trees are as rare as cavities constructed in trees other than pines. The birds almost always locate the cavities in the main trunks just below the lowest limbs. Since they are excavating hard living tissue, the length of time necessary increases substantially. The shortest period in which a bird is known to have initiated and completed a cavity is six months. Some cavities have required as long as two years for completion, but most seem to require at least a year to complete. This lengthy investment of time in a vital structure is unique.

The red-cockaded woodpecker's predilection for live pine trees begs explanation. Why should only one of the 21 kinds of woodpeckers in the United States resort to excavating a roosting and nesting cavity in living pine trees only? It is not the only woodpecker that frequents almost exclusively coniferous forests. So do the white-headed woodpecker found in the coniferous forests of Washington, Oregon, and California, the three-toed and black-backed woodpeckers that inhabit the boreal forests of spruce and fir, and the Williamson's and red-breasted sapsuckers inhabiting the pine forests of the western states. None of these birds undertakes the

FIGURE 4-1 Older red-cockaded woodpecker cavities are surrounded by a bare faceplate where bark has been completely removed during resin well maintenance.

tedious task of excavating a living pine tree.

Perhaps the excavation is not all that difficult. Certainly removal of the bark to reveal the underlying white sapwood is relatively easy. Also, we consider conifers to be "softwood" in comparison with many of the deciduous "hardwood" trees, such as oaks, hickories, etc. But "hard" and "soft" are relative terms, and while we can say the white pines of the Northeast are "soft," the southern yellow pines, such as longleaf, loblolly, slash, and shortleaf pines used by the bird, are considerably harder. So we can reasonably assume that the long period required for a red-cockaded woodpecker to complete a cavity has to do with how hard it is to penetrate the sapwood. This long excavation period is so characteristic of the species that we have a special term for the tree. We call any tree in which a red-cockaded woodpecker has begun to excavate a new cavity a start tree to indicate that birds have started to work on it. Once the horizontal entrance tunnel is complete and the vertical chamber is large enough for a bird to roost within, the tree will be designated a cavity tree. This is very simple, but very important, terminology, as we shall learn later.

Even the earliest chroniclers noted that red-cockaded woodpeckers select trees which have been attacked by a fungal infection known as red heart or heartrot. Some biologists have asserted that the fungal infection is essential to the successful completion of the cavity. The fungus, *Phellinus pini*, cannot successfully invade living sapwood, the white outermost layer of the tree beneath the bark. Tiny hollow tubes in the sapwood, called tracheids, transport fluids between the crowns and roots of trees. As trees grow, other cells, outside the tracheids, send minute growths through tiny pits in the tracheid walls. These growths block off the flow of water and the dissolved substances it carries to the upper portion of the tree. Because of this blockage, resins, gums, and pigments accumulate in the blocked tracheids and darken the color of the wood in the center of the tree. This distinct region, called heartwood, thereafter functions only to provide strength and support to the trunk of the tree. The tracheids of the heart-wood also traverse each of the limbs of the tree. When a branch of the tree breaks off, as in a windstorm, for example, the tracheids are exposed and susceptible to invasion by spores of the fungus. The digestive enzymes of the fungus allow it to eat its way through the tracheids and reach the heartwood of the trunk, where the fungus can spread both upward and downward in the trunk. Initially the heartwood remains firm, but as the fungal infection grows, the hard tra-cheids become soft masses of cellulose. These are the zones of soft tissue that the red-cockaded woodpecker can exploit when excavating a roost or nest chamber.

Pines, like humans and other organisms, become more vul-nerable to infectious diseases as they age. Several studies have verified that older trees have a much greater incidence of red heart infection than younger trees. Loblolly pines rarely con-tract red heart until they reach 60 years of age, shortleaf pines remain healthy until the age of 80, and longleaf pines even longer. Since red heart infection significantly reduces the commercial value of the tree, foresters prefer to harvest the tree before infection sets in. This practice results in fewer infected trees and a more rapid turnover in harvested trees, both beneficial results from the forester's viewpoint, but de-trimental to the red-cockaded woodpecker. Observers have frequently noted that red-cockaded woodpeckers generally lo-cate their cavities in the largest and oldest trees in the forest stand.

Intrigued by this unique woodpecker behavior, researchers have framed their questions to narrow down the potential explanations. Have the woodpeckers selected the largest trees because they are most likely to have infected heartwood? Have they selected the trees for other reasons and encounter the heartrot just because more large and old trees are in-fected? Can a woodpecker tell whether a tree has heartrot before it excavates all the way into the center? Can a woodpecker successfully complete a cavity in the absence of heart-rot? Answers have slowly emerged from the forest.

A study of cavity trees in a loblolly pine forest in Missis-sippi helped answer these questions. Researchers used a tool, called an increment borer, to cut a cylindrical piece of trunk about the size of a soda straw from the bark into the center of the tree, in an effort to determine if red heart was present in a tree at cavity height. They examined 200 cavity trees, and 75 percent of them had obvious red heart infections. This find-ing demonstrated that red-cockaded woodpeckers can exca-vate cavities in the absence of red heart infections. While it may be difficult to detect the earliest stages of infection with a core sample, certainly not all the cavities in the 25 percent of trees without obvious signs of red heart would have been infected.

The researchers also cored 40 nearby trees which had nei-ther cavities nor start holes. None had visible signs of red heart. This is curious because we would expect about 30, or 75 percent, of them to be infected. Did these trees differ in some way from those selected as potential cavity trees by the woodpeckers? It turns out that they did. While all the trees were of equal average height, they were not all of the same age and trunk width. The 40 trees ignored by the woodpeckers averaged 68 years of age and 19 inches in diameter (as mea-sured 4.5 feet above ground level). The uninfected cavity trees averaged 71 years of age and 25 inches in diameter, while the infected cavity trees averaged 77 years old and 23 inches in diameter. There were no large, old trees in the stand that the woodpeckers had not utilized as potential cavity trees. Wood-peckers seem to prefer wider trees, perhaps knowing they are older and more likely to have heartrot.

What can we conclude from this information? It appears that the rate of red heart infection increases rapidly as the trees reach seventy years and older. While infection will not cause a tree to shrink in diameter, it may cause them to grow less rapidly and result in trees of smaller diameter for a given age. But are the woodpeckers selecting infected trees, or are all old trees infected?

Red-cockaded woodpeckers had initiated work on 615 cavities in that Mississippi forest under study. But 387 were only start holes, and 55 percent of these start trees had red heart infections. The woodpeckers had completed 228 cavities; 73 percent had red heart, 10 percent showed no sign of red heart, and 17 percent were of uncertain status. These results raise an interesting prospect. Have the woodpeckers been able to identify which trees have red heart and abandon work on those which do not? Do the woodpeckers drill into the trees far enough for cavity enlargement and then abandon those where the going is too tough—that is, where they fail to find red heart—or do the woodpeckers provide a site for infection of the heartwood by the red heart fungus, with the birds returning some months later to excavate the soft, newly infected wood?

This study, like all good research, answered some questions and raised new ones. We have learned that the woodpeckers can indeed carve out a cavity in sound heartwood, but they prefer disease-weakened heartwood wherever possible. We also know that red heart fungus can infect pine trees without the assistance of the woodpeckers. We do not know if woodpecker excavations actively promote fungal infection.

Since the red-cockaded woodpecker is an endangered species and its cavity trees appear to play a vital role in its continued presence in the forests, we cannot run around cutting down cavity trees to pursue the interesting relationship between woodpecker and fungus. But an enterprising study in Texas has exploited natural tree death to address the question. It examined cavity trees which had died from fire, southern pine beetles, or windstorms. Red-cockaded woodpeckers rarely continue to use a tree once it has died, although other animals do, so removal of these dead trees did not hinder the lives of the endangered birds. The researchers cut free the section of the tree trunk containing the cavity. A vertical cut then exposed the center of the tree and cavity. They removed chips of heartwood aseptically and placed them on growth chemicals to culture and identify any fungi which were present. Red heart fungus typically grows along the tracheids in thin, vertical columns. Older infections have more and larger-diameter columns. A woodpecker excavating into infected heartwood would interrupt these vertical columns. If the infections began after the bird excavated the cavity, the pattern of infection would be different.

The study involved 34 trees with 51 cavities and 16 start holes. Nearly two-thirds (63 percent) of the cavities but less than half (44 percent) of the start holes were in trees with red heart infections at the level of excavation. This study confirmed that red heart infection is not a prerequisite for successful cavity completion. The study also hinted (without statistical proof), once again, that the woodpeckers may abort their excavation efforts if they do not encounter decay. Unfortunately the study did not gather data on the prevalence of red heart infection in the surrounding forest, and information from other sites and years was too variable to be helpful. The study did reveal that longleaf pine is more resistant to red heart infection than other species. Red heart decay afflicted 39 percent of 18 longleaf pine trees, 85 percent of 13 shortleaf pines, and all of the three loblolly pines examined. These data agree with more extensive studies of red heart infections in pines. It appears that pine gum, which contains oleoresins, protects tree wounds from fungi invasion. The copious production of pine gum is characteristic of longleaf pines. Red heart fungi seem unable to invade longleaf pines successfully until the trees are a hundred years old and gum production declines.

This study did help resolve the question of whether or not red-cockaded woodpecker excavations allowed heartrot fungus to infect trees. In all cases where the origin of the decay could be determined, infection started in the stub of a broken branch, not an entrance tunnel or chamber excavated by the birds. In fact, none of the 67 cavity entrance tubes or start holes showed any signs of fungus. As excavation proceeded, pine gum concentrated in the area and saturated the sapwood, effectively blocking out fungal spores. Heartwood is dead tissue and does not saturate with pine gum. This is critical, of course, for if heartwood did yield pine gum, it would soon fill a cavity and render it unsuitable for the woodpeckers.

To summarize, it appears that red-cockaded woodpeckers begin to excavate cavities with no knowledge of whether the interior heartwood has red heart infection or not. They are more likely to complete a cavity if they do find red heart decay but are quite capable of finishing the chamber in firm heartwood if need be. Their excavations do not promote the introduction of red heart fungi into the tree. Older trees, which are more likely to contain fungal decay, are more suitable as potential cavity trees. Unfortunately, modern forestry techniques, which seek to shorten the growth to harvest interval and remove large trees before the onset of fungal infections, will eventually eliminate the larger, older, infected trees favored by the woodpecker.

There is another aspect of red-cockaded woodpecker cavities that is even more intriguing than the heartwood connection. We have already seen that pines can produce copious amounts of pine gum, or pitch, which contains oleoresins. Pines contain resin canals scattered throughout much of the sapwood. These canals are lined with specialized cells that secrete resin into the canal cavities. This resin is a combination of a liquid solvent called turpentine and a waxy substance called rosin. When a tree is wounded or damaged by insects, the resin quickly flows to and covers the area, sometimes trapping the insects since resin is very sticky. Once exposed to the air, the turpentine component evaporates quickly, leaving behind a protective layer of rosin, which prevents water loss and fungal invasion. This physiological process is the basis for a large and economically significant naval stores industry in the southeastern states, especially Georgia and Florida. The term "naval stores" originally applied to the tars, pitch, and timber used to build and maintain wooden sailing ships. Today it refers to pitch products obtained from pine trees. The most prodigious pitch producers, slash and longleaf pines, are systematically wounded at the base of the trunk to prompt the flow of resin, which is then gathered and distilled to separate the turpentine from the rosin. Both turpentine and rosin have several industrial uses and find their way into soap, detergent, paint, varnish, lacquer, ink, shoe polish, linoleum, and roofing materials.

Certain woodpeckers have exploited the sap as a resource for thousands of years. The yellow-breasted sapsucker drills a horizontal row of small holes around a tree trunk, deep enough to penetrate the sapwood and initiate the flow of sap. Using a bristled tongue tip, the bird drinks this sap for the sugars it contains. The sap also attracts insects, which adhere to its sticky surface. In effect, the sapsuckers establish a tree farm. They drill the sap wells and repeatedly circulate among the trees to drink the fresh sap and eat the trapped insects. Sapsuckers thus established traplines and sap-gathering rituals long before humans invented traps or discovered the sweet rewards of maple trees in the springtime.

Sapsuckers also dig wells in pine trees. This raises a curious question. The sap flows through the tree in those tiny straws, the tracheids. Resin flows in larger canals paralleling, and immediately adjacent to, the sap-containing tracheids. While the desirability of sugar-containing sap is understandable, the resin, which contains turpentine and oleoresins, is surely less palatable. Do sapsuckers revisit holes that yield sap but abandon those that tapped resin canals?

Red-cockaded woodpeckers are not known to drink pine sap or harvest sap-entrapped insects. Nor are they satisfied with dainty little sap holes. These woodpeckers want full flow or nothing. Naturally, as a red-cockaded woodpecker begins to drill with a cavity in mind, the pine resin starts to flow as soon as the bark is penetrated and the sapwood breached. The golden sap ebbs stickily down the tree trunk. Fresh drops of sap in full sunlight sparkle like gems. As the turpentine evaporates, the sap turns white and stands out against the gray-brown of the tree trunk. This is the key that ground-ridden biologists use to locate cavity trees. One would think that this sap would be quite a nuisance. It certainly is bother-some to the biologists ascending the tree trunks. But one dribble of pine pitch on the trunk does not satisfy the wood-peckers. They deliberately excavate other holes above, below, and to the side of the cavity entrance. These wounds are not deep into the trunk, however. They serve only to produce pitch. The wounds receive frequent attention from the wood-peckers, which work them over regularly and maintain a con-stant flow of resin. In time the amount of resin exuded from these wells can completely cover the tree trunk above and below the cavity entrance for some distance. Some old cavity trees appear almost white and are very conspicuous in the forest.

This resin well drilling is curious behavior. No other wood-pecker does anything like this. It also is very expensive behav-ior in terms of energy consumption. Not only do the birds excavate numerous resin wells, but they must tend to each frequently, almost on a daily basis. Moreover, the woodpeck-ers do not drill resin wells just on the cavity tree. Frequently they excavate wells on other trees surrounding the cavity tree. It is common to see a pair of woodpeckers return at dusk to their roost cavities, which may be in the same tree or two trees not far apart. The female may dally a bit in the neighborhood before retiring for the evening. But without fail the male con-scientiously will make the rounds of the resin wells, vigorously reopening the wounds to maintain resin flow, before popping into his cavity. Both birds may tend to the wells during off hours of the day when they are not foraging for food.

Interestingly, red-breasted nuthatches have similar behav-ior. These birds carry droplets of pitch from pine, spruce, and balsam fir trees to their nests, which may be in hardwood trees or even birdhouses. Both sexes smear the pitch generously all about the opening to the nest, especially at the bottom, occasionally covering an area up to several inches from the opening. Some observers have reported pitch smeared within the entrance tunnel as well. Just as the red-cockaded woodpecker is the only woodpecker that utilizes pitch at its nest, so the red-breasted nuthatch is the only nuthatch known to carry pitch to its nest site. Since nuthatches can excavate a cavity only in deadwood, it is unable to make use of the natural flow of pitch in a living pine, as the red-cockaded woodpecker manages to do.

As one might expect, the continual working of the resin wells can produce more than minor damage to the tree. The tree is particularly vulnerable where the resin wells are closest together, the area immediately surrounding the entrance to the woodpecker cavity. In time, damage from the wells may be sufficient to kill the cambium tissue, ending the production of new bark layers completely. It is common to find red-cockaded woodpecker cavities surrounded by bare deadwood devoid of any bark for a distance of several inches from the entrance. We call such a bare zone around the entrance a cavity plate. As a cavity plate forms, the woodpeckers continue to open new resin wells as close to the entrance as possible. Should the damage become so extreme that resin ceases to flow around the cavity entrance, the woodpeckers will abandon the cavity. If the tree should die for any reason, such as fire, lightning, disease, pine beetle infestations, the birds abandon the tree when the sap ceases to flow.

As you might imagine, people have offered all sorts of explanations for this behavior. Some have suggested that the gum-whitened tree trunk acts as a signpost, assisting the birds in distinguishing their cavity tree from the many look-alike

FIGURE 4-2 Drips and dribbles of resin and rosin coat the treetrunk surrounding the cavity entrance.

trees in the forest. This view seems to reflect the inadequacies of biologists more than those of birds. Wild animals seem to find their way in the forest much more skillfully than biologists, who are forever getting lost. Many species, including the red-cockaded woodpecker, also occupy a limited defended territory with which they become intimately familiar, so that a distinctive signpost would appear unnecessary. It also seems antithetical to other animal behaviors, particularly the efforts of most animals to disguise the locations of their nests, rather than advertise them. Surely a bird would have to devise a predatorproof nest before boldly advertising it to the world. While we could probably test this orientation hypothesis, perhaps by painting the whitened trunk to match the surrounding trees and observing the behavior of the residents, few biologists have considered it worth the effort.

A more intriguing suggestion holds that the sticky resin acts to deter predators or competitors for the nest cavity. This hypothesis has fallen in and out of favor as various observers have noted that the presence of fresh resin at the entrance of the cavity seldom seems to be deter other woodpeckers, other birds, and mammals such as flying squirrels. Certainly extensive areas of resin on the trunk would not be useful in deterring birds, which fly directly to the cavity entrance. If the resin acts as a deterrent, it must protect the nest against an interloper that would climb the tree trunk. Squirrels are the most likely mammals to usurp the cavities. Fox, gray, and flying squirrels share the pine forests at various localities. All these squirrels are common in the forest, seem quite at home in pine trees and often construct nests in them, shred pinecones to eat the seeds within, and hardly seem likely to back away from a little pine resin.

One group of predators remains that seems highly unlikely to pose a threat to woodpeckers: snakes. If ever there was a creature that seemed destined to remain earthbound, particularly in a forest of towering, straight-trunked pine trees, it must be the snake. But there is one particular snake, the rat snake, that commonly inhabits pine forests and does not appear to have read the book. It comes in a variety of colors, such as yellow, gray, and black, and ranges from four to six feet in length when fully grown. It also likes to climb trees and eat birds, their nestlings, and their eggs. It can not only climb trees but does it the hard way: no sissified techniques here, crawling into low, multibranched shrubs or coiling around trunks of small diameter. The rat snake will approach a towering pine tree of substantial girth and proceed to crawl right up the trunk, nearly as straight as a stick. It secures with its belly scales a solid grip on the rough bark of the vertical trunk, and up it goes. It may take advantage of a vertical crevice in the bark, if available, to gain a little side leverage, but otherwise it just climbs straight up.

Biologists have found rat snakes in red-cockaded woodpecker cavities by poking into the holes with battery-powered flashlight bulbs and oversize dental mirrors. They have even seen the snakes entering the cavities to prey on unsuspecting flying squirrels. One biologist observed a snake enter a red-cockaded woodpecker nest, eat the nestlings, and remain in the cavity for nine days, digesting its meal and occasionally poking its head out. These observations hardly lend credence to the hypothesis that red-cockaded woodpeckers maintain the resin wells to repel predacious snakes.

Serendipitous observations of snakes climbing cavity trees, entering cavities, and even consuming cavity inhabitants titillate the curiosity of field observers. But they do not yield adequate data to resolve the inconsistencies of the observations. A Mississippi State University biologist, Jerry Jackson, grabbed the bull by the horns, or, more accurately, the snake by the neck, and moved the observations into a controlled laboratory situation. He first captured a number of gray rat snakes and established them in captivity. Then, in an escape-proof test area, he set up two vertical loblolly pine logs and installed a wooden box with suitable entrance holes on top of each log. He placed the snakes in the test area and periodically checked them. If they had climbed a log to reach the cover provided by the boxes, he placed them back down on the ground. The snakes tested showed no hesitation to climb the logs to reach the cover provided by the boxes.

Then Jackson smeared a two-inch-wide ring of pine gum around one of the logs. To his surprise, the snakes continued to reach the box atop the log with pine gum, but none had any pine gum smeared on its body. Further observations revealed that the snakes were carefully arching their bodies over the pine gum to avoid direct contact with it. To counter their clever evasion, Jackson then smeared a broader band of pine gum on the log. Most of the snakes avoided the gummed log but continued to climb the clean one. He found those snakes that did climb the gummed log writhing on the floor of the cage in obvious discomfort, attempting to keep the smeared portions of their bodies from touching anything. The snake with the most gum on its body died. Jackson subsequently stopped applying fresh gum to the log. As the gum dried up, the snakes resumed climbing the log.

This experiment explains the inconsistencies between the hypothesis that resin deters predators and the observations of successful predation. Rat snakes climb exceptionally well and show no hesitation to do so. Fresh pine resin is very irritating to them and can, in sufficient quantities, cause death. Dried pine rosin has little, if any, value as a deterrent. Animals that usurp red-cockaded woodpecker cavities, but do not maintain the flow of resin from the resin wells, are susceptible to snake predation. When resin wells around a cavity entrance dry up and no longer provide protection, the woodpeckers will abandon the cavity. This experiment also helps us understand why the woodpeckers dig resin wells on trees surrounding the cavity tree. Cavities generally sit just below the lowest branches on the trunk. When trees grow close together, as they typically do, the branches of one tree provide access to the branches of adjacent trees. One has only to watch squirrels methodically and quickly traverse a forest through the treetops to realize what a marvelous transportation network the trees provide. Rat snakes could ascend trees without resin wells and quickly cross over to the cavity tree just above the entrance hole to the cavity. Red-cockaded woodpeckers seem to be more clever than we generally appreciate.

Fifteen years later three researchers (Craig Rudolph, Howard Kyle, and Richard Conner) in Texas extended this inquiry by taking rat snakes outdoors to real woodpecker cavity trees. Using 9 rat snakes 2 to 6 feet long, they tested the ability of the snakes to climb normal pine trees as well as resin-coated cavity trees. Of 63 attempts to climb noncavity tree trunks, 62 were successful. Only 3 of 18 attempts to climb cavity trees were successful. The 3 successful ascents were performed by the 2 smallest snakes, which were able to insinuate their bodies into small fissures between adjacent bark plates. Larger snakes climbed slowly, spent more time seeking an acceptable route up the tree, and occasionally fell from the trees.

Red-cockaded woodpeckers typically scale flakes of bark off the surfaces of their cavity trees so that the tree trunks become rather smooth. The fissures in the bark gradually fill with resin over the years so that the tree trunk becomes even smoother, without crevices, and coated with sticky resin. Examination of the snakes revealed that small amounts of pine resin adhered to their belly scales. Even tiny dabs of resin interfered with the movement of adjoining belly scales. Since the sequential movement of ventral scales is what propels snakes forward, the resulting loss of mobility was sufficient to prevent ascension of the tree. The woodpeckers have a multipronged defense that really works.

Still unanswered are questions about how the rat snakes came to develop their climbing abilities and why the woodpeckers began excavating in live pine trees. Some people have suggested that the frequency of fires in the pine forests may have initiated both. Rat snakes that had climbing skills would be more likely to survive a ground fire. Dead trees would be more likely to catch fire and burn completely. This hypothesis is interesting but not compelling. Snakes that do not climb are also common in the pine forests, as are woodpeckers that nest in dead trees. While living pine trees with thick protective bark do survive fires remarkably well, very old cavity trees, with layers of flammable pine rosin coating the trunk, can turn into veritable torches should the flames reach the rosin.

One further characteristic of red-cockaded woodpecker cavities has received a great deal of attention. While the entrance to an individual cavity can face any conceivable compass point, as a group they are predominantly oriented toward the west. Naturalist John Dennis was the first to notice this phenomenon, after studying 362 cavities in northeastern South Carolina. Since this characteristic is easy to measure, other workers quickly verified the feature in other regions. Wildlife biologists Melvin Hopkins and Teddy Lynn measured 562 trees elsewhere in South Carolina with similar results; naturalists Harley Jones and Frederick Ott studied 119 cavities in Georgia and found even stronger westward tendencies, while biologist Wilson Baker examined 149 trees in Florida that favored a southwest orientation. As shown in Figure 4-1, opposite, completed cavities and start holes may face any direction, but far more often than not, they tend to face the west. Differences among study sites appear when cavity orientations are grouped into eight compass points as in the figure, but overall, west is best.

This phenomenon spawned an interest in nest orientation among woodpecker students. Speculation and additional measurements erupted at sporadic intervals for a decade. Was the phenomenon real? Did it hold across the entire range of the woodpecker? How on earth did it function? Ornithologists Brian Locke and Richard Conner finally summarized the mass of data available for 3,354 cavities across the entire range of the bird. They demonstrated statistically that the orientation of the cavities is not random, even though any

COMPASS ORIENTATION OF
CAVITIES AND START HOLES

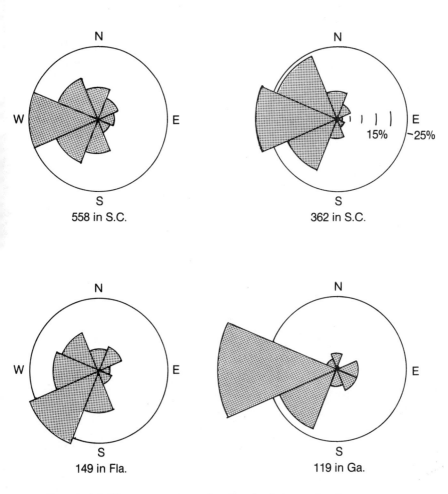

FIGURE 4-3 The proportion of red-cockaded woodpecker cavities and start holes which face the cardinal and intermediate compass directions at four localities, with predominant west and southwest orientation.

given cavity can face any direction. Although there is considerable variation everywhere, the average orientation in the east (North and South Carolina, Florida) was 271 degrees, one degree from due west, 270 degrees; in the west (Oklahoma and Texas) it was 272 degrees. Whatever influences the direction that the entrance to a cavity faces, it operates wherever the species lives.

Since a cavity can face virtually any direction no matter where it is found, could it be that some unknown factor influences which cavities woodpeckers actually complete? We know that cavities require one or two years of construction. This would certainly be ample time for some unknown factor to cancel the project along the way. We also know that start holes, which represent unfinished cavities, are quite common. Woodpeckers abandon many start holes for lengthy periods, if not forever. Perhaps woodpeckers initiate start holes in random directions but for some reason finish only holes with certain qualities.

Two sets of data allow us to test the hypothesis that woodpeckers start holes randomly but complete them nonrandomly. Wildlife biologist Don Wood examined 155 cavity trees in southeastern Oklahoma and found 343 excavations. Twenty percent of the excavations had not progressed to the cavity stage when he measured them. Grouping the data into the 16 principal compass directions shown in Figure 4-2, opposite, we see that the orientation of the completed cavities is very similar to the orientation of the initial start holes.

Data which I collected on 168 excavations in South Carolina produced similar results. Neither the initial excavations nor the completed cavities were randomly oriented. The average direction of the initial excavations was 287 degrees, or west-north-west; that of the completed cavities was 276 degrees, nearly due west. Forty-five percent of the excavations were unfinished when measured, more than twice the fraction found in Oklahoma. The slight difference in orientation between the initial excavations (start holes) and the final prod-

COMPASS ORIENTATION OF INITIAL
STARTS AND COMPLETED CAVITIES

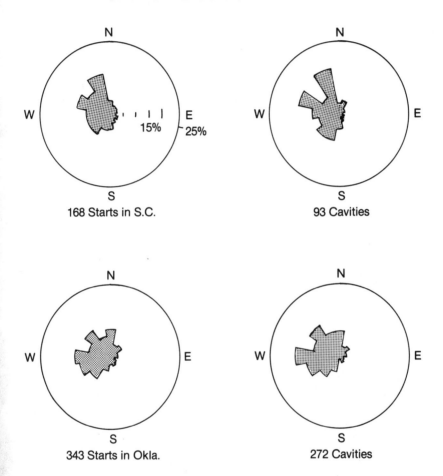

FIGURE 4-4 The directional orientation of start holes (left) and completed cavities (right) in South Carolina (upper) and Oklahoma (lower).

ucts (completed cavities) had no statistical significance. We can therefore say that woodpeckers do not commence excavation in random directions and, because of some unknown factor, finish only cavities facing west. Whatever the influencing factor may be, it seems to exert its effect from the very beginning. We must reject our hypothesis.

The tendency for red-cockaded woodpeckers to favor a westerly exposure for their cavities is certainly real. Why this should be so has spawned a great deal of speculation. Before proceeding to that subject, however, we need to address another question: Does the orientation of red-cockaded cavities differ from that of other woodpecker species?

Biologists have not investigated the orientation of other woodpecker cavities as intensively as that of the red-cockaded woodpecker. Louise Lawrence studied the cavities of four woodpecker species in central Ontario and found that openings facing east to south were most common. Among 42 cavities of yellow-bellied sapsuckers, she found that 15 faced south, 6 southeast, 8 east, and 8 west; the average direction was toward the south, approximately 173 degrees. Of 25 northern flicker nests, 21 also faced south, southeast, or east, averaging approximately 116 degrees, or ESE. She found only 11 nests each for the hairy and downy woodpeckers, too few to infer reliable conclusions, but they ranged from east to south to west.

David Inouye found similar orientation in Colorado, where 36 yellow-bellied sapsucker cavities faced from northeast around the compass to northwest, averaging 170 degrees; none faced northward. A half dozen northern flicker nests faced southeast, south, or southwest, averaging 182 degrees. Allen Crockett and Harlo Hadow examined 57 Williamson's sapsucker nests and 51 red-naped sapsucker nests in Colorado and Wyoming and reported that 57 percent opened southward while only 18 percent opened northward. Richard Conner studied 78 nests of six species in Virginia and found that more cavities faced northeast (29) or southeast (24) than southwest (12) or northwest (13). The 22 northern flicker nests he found showed the most uniform orientation, with 13 of 22 facing northeast. Only Ann Reller, in Illinois, found woodpecker cavities that tended to face westward, with 10 red-headed woodpecker nests averaging 267 degrees, almost due west, and 7 red-bellied woodpecker nests averaging 225 degrees, or southwest.

These studies indicate several generalities. Most woodpeckers, like the red-cockaded, excavate holes facing almost any direction, but none of them, as an aggregate, has a random orientation. While it is always possible to calculate average directions, the amount of variation for any given species is horrendous. Furthermore, unlike the thousands of red-cockaded woodpecker cavities that have been examined, nobody has studied other species in sufficient quantity and at enough different localities across their geographic range to draw any firm conclusions. However, none of the other species seems to prefer the westerly exposure typical of the red-cockaded woodpeckers.

Why should it make any difference which way a woodpecker hole faces? What advantage does any given orientation have over any other direction? Most hypotheses focus on three factors: sun, wind, and lean of the tree. A nest with eastern exposure will receive rays from the morning, presumably warming sun. A nest with a southward orientation will get sunshine for the greater part of the day. A western exposure will experience the greatest amount of heating. The benefits to be gained will differ from summer to winter and with the amount of shading from adjacent trees, which also varies seasonally. If there is a prevailing wind direction, the wind could be cooling in summer but chilling in winter. If the trunk or limb containing the cavity is not exactly vertical, it will present a "top side" and "bottom side." This lean becomes important for rain entering the cavity entrance, water running down the trunk of the tree, and predators or nest hole competitors gaining access to the cavity.

Louise Lawrence, working in chilly Ontario, thought that the light and warmth entering cavities facing east and south might be the compelling reason for favoring these exposures. The sapsucker nests in Colorado and Wyoming that faced south seem to support this hypothesis. However, the valley where David Inouye conducted his study ran north-south, and 39 of the 42 cavities he found were on the east side of the valley, where the early-morning sun did not reach them. In Virginia the prevailing wind was southwest, and the cavities found by Richard Conner tended to face northeast. He demonstrated, however, that the cavities were almost invariably on the "underside" of the tree trunk and argued that the slope of the trunk was the dominant factor in nest orientation, a view that helps explain the great variation in the weak preference for any one direction found in all these studies.

If an east or southerly exposure is preferable in a cool or cold climate, then one might expect some shift in orientation in a hot environment. This is exactly what David and Richard Inouye and Nancy Huntly found in the Arizona desert. There the Gila woodpecker excavates cavities in the tall saguaro cactus. The researchers examined 49 cavities and found that while once again, individual cavities can face any direction, as a group the average direction was 351 degrees, nearly due north. Saguaro cavities receive the full brunt of the hot desert sun. The investigators hypothesized that if this nonrandom orientation was an adaptive response to the environment, two criteria must be met: The microclimate within the nest must be influenced by the orientation of the nest, and this influence must be advantageous to the birds. Earlier studies had shown that temperatures inside both north-facing and south-facing nests were cooler than air temperatures during the heat of the day. Furthermore, north-facing nests were consistently cooler than south-facing nests during both winter and summer. This could benefit the birds in two ways. In the summer birds, especially nestlings, in a north-facing cavity would be cooler and not lose as much water. In the winter birds that roosted in a south-facing cavity would be warmer and spend less energy just keeping warm.

Since most woodpeckers excavate several cavities a year, there is usually a surplus of cavities available. This surplus provides alternative hideaways for birds threatened by predators, ready-made shelters for juveniles when they learn to fly, and other purposes. Orientation studies typically record the direction cavities face without consideration of their current occupancy status. The Gila woodpeckers provide an interesting, albeit labor-intensive, opportunity for further research. Do these woodpeckers occupy north-facing cavities during the warm months and shift to south-facing cavities during the winter?

What we are facing with all these studies is the difficulty in providing unambiguous explanations to ambiguous circumstances. We see tendencies in the data, not exclusive behavior. Several factors could influence a woodpecker's choice of sites for excavation and choice of cavities for occupancy under varying environmental conditions. We could perhaps arrive at a resolution of the ambiguities through experimentation. But how can one experiment with woodpecker excavation behavior?

Thomas Grubb and his colleagues have provided some answers to this dilemma by using a simple but ingenious technique: Provide the birds with artificial trees. They have used polystyrene cylinders about 9 inches in diameter, painted brown, and placed in woodlots or recently clearcut wooded areas. Sixteen sets of 3 cylinders—4 feet, 8 feet, and 12 feet high—were set out in the woods. Downy woodpeckers excavated cavities in 16 of the cylinders. Males preferred the taller posts and excavated closer to the top of the posts than females. The 8-foot posts were the most popular. Next, the researchers placed fifty 8-foot posts 75 yards apart in woodlots. Over the next 11 months, downy woodpeckers excavated 51 cavities in 42 of the posts, using all as roost holes. The prevailing wind at the site was from the southwest. The

22 cavities excavated from November through March faced away from the wind, averaging 72 degrees. The 29 cavities excavated from April through September faced random directions, averaging 126 degrees. Since there was negligible lean to any of the cylinders, it appears that wind was the main factor influencing entrance orientation.

Grubb and his co-workers then placed 99 polystyrene "snag tree" posts in a clearcut area adjacent to a mature forest in Ohio. The artificial trees were again 8 feet high, but this time they had square sides, oriented with the sides facing the cardinal directions. The downy woodpeckers thus had to choose an entrance that would face north, east, south, or west. Although the researchers planted the posts in vertical positions, 68 of them subsequently leaned toward one side. Over the course of a year, from October to the next September, downy woodpeckers excavated 31 of the 34 cavities created. Although only two-thirds of the posts were leaning, the birds drilled 82 percent (28 of 34) of their cavities in leaning posts, and 86 percent (24 of 28) of these cavities were on the underside of the leaning post.

The prevailing wind at this site came from the southwest. As for direction, 12 of the cavities faced north, 8 to the east, 14 to the west, but none faced south. The average direction was 333 degrees, or NNW. Although 10 of the 99 posts erected had a southward lean, only 1 had been excavated, and that cavity was not on the southern, or underside, of the post. Because the researchers limited the options available to the woodpeckers, the south side was left completely unexcavated. The season had no effect on orientation of the cavity entrance. The birds made 6 north-facing cavities during the winter, 6 in summer; 4 east cavities in winter, 4 in summer; 6 west cavities in winter, 8 in summer. Once again we find it hard to obtain unambiguous answers to our queries. The lean of the post determined the orientation of most of the cavities. However, the woodpeckers avoided completely all posts leaning to the south. Cavities facing north and east enjoyed shelter from the prevailing southwest wind, but entrances facing west were most common. Both east and west cavities received sunlight, but the full exposure of southern entrances attracted no woodpeckers. The downy woodpeckers were obviously not seeking sunlight, did not much care about where the winds came from, and while they preferred the undersides of leaning posts, that was not the sole factor influencing their choice of location.

What have we learned from these experiments and field studies? These relatively low artificial trees attract downy woodpeckers more readily than other species. However, we do not know how these cavities in artificial trees compare with downy woodpecker cavities in real trees in the area. Lawrence found that this species avoided NW, N, or NE entrances in Ontario. Conner found NE, SE, and NW cavities in Virginia, but only 1 of 19 faced SW. No woodpecker, other than the red-cockaded, shows any uniformity in excavation, and the same species may vary from one geographic area to another. This makes the consistent west or southwest orientation demonstrated by red-cockaded woodpeckers wherever they live even more striking.

Now we return to the first question: Why do red-cockaded woodpecker nests face west? We have seen that the lean of the tree has influenced the direction that nests of other species face. Most other woodpeckers excavate in dead tree trunks or limbs and frequently place their cavities near the tops of the limbs or trunks. It is uncommon for such limbs to be perfectly vertical; therefore, given a choice, the birds place their cavities on the undersides of the limbs. The cavities seem to lodge in the thinnest available limbs or trunks, possibly to prevent larger birds from appropriating and enlarging the cavities. The red-cockaded woodpecker virtually always places its cavity in the main trunk of the tree immediately below the lowest limbs. The tree seldom has any significant lean at this point, so it is unlikely that the lean of the trunk has anything to do with cavity entrance orientation.

Winds can either cool cavity occupants in summer or chill them in winter. But the westward orientation seems constant from the Atlantic shoreline to east Texas, the full range of the species. It is unlikely that prevailing winds are consistent over this thousand-mile expanse.

The third factor frequently mentioned as a potential influence on cavity orientation is the sun, which provides both heat and light. Woodpeckers typically exit their roost cavities at or shortly after daybreak and do not retire until dusk, except during inclement weather. Therefore, the thought that sunlight entering the cavity influences its orientation is not too appealing. The entrance tunnel is sufficiently deep, and slanted upward, to prevent rays from the midday sun from entering the cavity directly.

The second component of sunshine is heat. Would early-morning sunlight penetrating the cavity provide an extra dollop of heat on a cold winter morning? Perhaps, but the birds have usually left the cavity before the heat could be significant. They are generating body heat through the muscular activity of flying and foraging. Besides, sunshine will reach westward-facing cavities in the afternoon, not morning. The birds seldom retire until after the sun has set and darkness is falling, so they are unlikely to derive benefit from the evening sun either. The sun is heating the surface of the tree throughout the day, however. Could this be the key to the riddle?

Recall that red-cockaded woodpeckers dig resin wells on their cavity trees and tend them nearly daily. For a long time people have suggested that westward orientation of the cavities exploits the effect of prolonged exposure to the sun on the flow of resin down the tree trunk. Sunlight heats the southern half of a tree trunk all day long. The trunk is coldest in the morning, having cooled throughout the night. Morning sunlight would augment resin flow, but the air temperature does not peak until midafternoon. The sun would have its greatest effect when the additional heat provided by direct sunlight combines with the highest air temperature. Interestingly, no one has ever tested this concept in the field through observations or experimentation. It would be easy to create artificial resin wells at intervals around the tree trunk and measure the flow of resin from each to determine if more resin flows from westerly wells than those facing other directions. The resin well hypothesis is a logical, but unproved, explanation for this phenomenon. Perhaps its appealing logic has inhibited testing of the concept since the results seem so obvious to all.

Thus far we have considered the red-cockaded woodpecker cavities only from the viewpoint of the bird. Cavities provide roosting holes, a nesting location, protection from predators and inclement weather—in other words, a useful home. But if the cavity provides these services to the excavator, could it not also provide them to other denizens of the forest? The red-cockaded woodpecker may be the only species with the fortitude and determination to excavate successfully in living pine trees, but once a cavity has been created, don't less capable species covet it as well? Indeed, they do.

Lester Short has termed the attention that cavities draw from other species as the "burden" of the woodpecker hole-excavating habit. The two hundred woodpecker species of the world must compete for their own cavities with thousands of other species, including other woodpeckers. It is no exaggeration to state that hundreds of species worldwide observe the excavation process with acquisitive intent and avail themselves of the first opportunity to dispossess the excavator. New cavities are particularly in demand, for they are clean and free of nest parasites and other vermin. The extent of this competition can occasionally be furious. Among woodpeckers that excavate cavities in dead limbs in a matter of days, some individual birds have had to excavate three or more cavities in succession, losing each of their new nests to aggressive competitors. Such losses can harm the woodpecker. Excavating another cavity, which requires time and energy, may inhibit reproduction by delaying it past the best time for feeding nestlings. If the female cannot delay egg laying, forcing the pair to occupy a less desirable old cavity, the eggs and hatchlings may be more vulnerable to predation or the danger of nest parasites.

Woodpeckers have evolved several tactics to help them cope with nest competition. As the cavity nears completion, at least one member of the mated pair remains close to the nest. Dislodging a woodpecker defending its cavity from within can be a painful, injurious task. The near-constant protection of the cavity, eggs, and hatchlings by the woodpecker pair until the young birds are large enough to "protect" themselves and the cavity makes eviction much less likely.

Making entrance holes and tunnels as small in diameter as possible is further defense against expropriation. Other woodpeckers have the capacity to enlarge a cavity entrance to accommodate their own dimensions; but many competitors do not, and these species must occupy a cavity "as is." If they cannot fit through the entrance, they cannot use the cavity. Many woodpeckers typically excavate in the smallest possible limb for similar reasons. Larger woodpeckers evicting a small species need to increase the size of the cavity. If the limb is not large enough to accommodate this, the large species will search elsewhere for a prefabricated home. Similarly, placing the entrance hole on the underside of a limb makes access even more difficult for nonwoodpecker competitors.

Woodpeckers are rather aggressive animals, and they tend to react violently to the presence of cavity competitors. Occasionally, however, two competing species can be found nesting, in separate cavities, in the same tree trunk. A few woodpeckers, especially those with omnivorous feeding habits, are also social species. Typical bark foragers must space themselves out to ensure adequate food supplies for all individuals. Omnivores can take advantage of locally abundant nuts or fruit and form social groups, even nesting in colonies. This results in more cooperating adults present in the vicinity of the nest or nests at all times, providing mutual protection for all the colonists.

How does the red-cockaded woodpecker fare in the struggle for nest sites? It has no shortage of competitors. Larger red-bellied and red-headed woodpeckers and flickers frequently usurp red-cockaded woodpecker cavities for roost and nest sites. Perhaps more onerous is the damage pileated woodpeckers inflict. These large birds seldom occupy red-cockaded woodpecker cavities, but they seem drawn to them as if by magnet. The pileateds enlarge the size of the entrance drastically in an unmistakable fashion. The red-cockaded cavity entrance is neat and symmetrical, an example of quality craftsmanship. The red-bellied and red-headed woodpeckers enlarge the entrance to accommodate their larger bodies, but the hole is still rather neat and symmetrical. The final product of pileated enlargement looks as if you or I had taken an ax to the entrance. It resembles how the front door of your home would look after police or firemen had made a forced entry—like a disaster. The end result is often unfit for occupancy even by squirrels or raccoons. The large, jagged hole freely admits rainfall, and a water-filled cavity suits only mosquitoes and treefrogs.

Eastern bluebirds have a great attraction to red-cockaded cavities when they are placed near open areas. In deeper woods, Carolina chickadees, tufted titmice, and white-breasted nuthatches are quick to take advantage of unoccupied cavities. If other woodpeckers have enlarged the entrance, crested flycatchers join the waiting line. Starlings also take over cavities. Flying squirrels are common occupants because they can squeeze through an unenlarged entrance, although they are capable of enlarging the entrance by gnawing. Once the entrances are enlarged, gray or fox squirrels are quick to establish housekeeping. Following remodeling by pileated woodpeckers, even raccoons can be accommodated. Finally, bees and wasps also lay claim to unoccupied cavities.

Some of these species occupy cavities one after another

within a single season. John Dennis has noted one cavity that was home first to red-cockadeds and then to flying squirrels. In the reverse direction, cavities occupied by flying squirrels subsequently housed red-cockaded and red-headed woodpeckers, flickers, crested flycatchers, gray squirrels, and honeybees. Clearly, cavity occupancy can be rather dynamic, with rapid turnover, especially of abandoned cavities.

We see that red-cockaded cavities are in high demand and that the woodpeckers provide a valuable service to many other species in the forest ecosystem. This service would be particularly valuable in predominantly pine forests where hardwood trees are scarce. Since no other species can excavate cavities in living pines, many cavity nesters depend almost solely upon the red-cockaded woodpecker for their reproductive success. Any attempt to evaluate the worth of red-cockaded woodpeckers to the total forest ecosystem must include as an indirect benefit the supply of cavities other species in the forest use as their homes.

Joe Skorupa once found a very unusual cavity tree on the Savannah River Plant in South Carolina. First, the loblolly pine tree had two trunks, which are rare. The trunks separated about 3 feet above the ground. There were two red-cockaded woodpecker cavities in this tree, one in each trunk. Second, this tree had retained its lower limbs for a long time, even though it had grown large in diameter. The large stubs of these limbs extended as low as 10 feet above the ground. Most pines of this size have no limbs on the lower half of the trunk. Both cavities were above the lowest limbs, unusual because red-cockaded woodpeckers typically excavate their cavities beneath the lowest limb of the pine. Furthermore, both trunks of the tree had died, apparently when a ground fire, a prescribed burn initiated by the U.S. Forest Service to control the growth of hardwoods in the area, burned too hot. A number of trees in the area were blackened far up their trunks.

One trunk of this tree had a cavity 29 feet above the

ground. The amount of old, dried, and silvered resin on the trunk above and below the cavity indicated that red-cockaded woodpeckers had used the tree for many years. When it was discovered in July, the cavity was occupied by a family of red-headed woodpeckers. The cavity entrance had been enlarged to 2 inches wide and 2½ inches high. The other trunk had a cavity 17 feet above the ground. A few old resin wells dotted the tree far above the cavity. These wells were at the same height as the cavity in the opposite trunk. Its former inhabitant probably had drilled and maintained them in conjunction with the original cavity. The lower cavity was unique. The entrance hole was perfectly formed and unenlarged, being 2 inches wide and 2 inches high, common for the species. A typical faceplate had been formed by removal of bark for several inches all around the entrance hole. An enormous number of resin wells had been drilled all over the trunk above and below the cavity, but not one drop of resin had exuded from any of the wells or the faceplate. An adult male red-cockaded woodpecker resided in this cavity. Another bird, perhaps a female, frequently accompanied this male, but its cavity tree was never located.

The red-headed woodpeckers appeared to have driven the male red-cockaded out of his cavity and nested there. The male red-cockaded then excavated a new cavity lower down in the adjacent trunk. Because both trunks had been killed by the fire, no resin was forthcoming anywhere on the trunk despite the numerous wells created by the male. Excavation of cavities in dead trees is extremely rare. The following January the male was still residing in the second cavity. The red-headed woodpeckers had moved on, not unusual because this species typically migrates away from this forest during the winter. The male red-cockaded had continued to work on both of the dead tree trunks, removing more bark from around the entrances, visibly enlarging the faceplates. Not one drop of resin could be seen. A start hole in a nearby live pine, initiated during the summer, or earlier, remained unfinished. This pair of birds raised no young that year and had disappeared completely by the following year. Competition for cavities can apparently have a severe impact on red-cockaded woodpecker survival.

Likewise, we must consider the effect of human activity on this intense competition for red-cockaded woodpecker cavities. Current management practice in the southeastern forests calls for complete removal of all trees at harvest and establishment of pine monoculture plantations. Fire and herbicides combine to eradicate hardwood sprouts and seedlings as the forest grows, meaning the "well-managed" forest will mature without hardwood trees. Except for a few dead pine branches, there will be no suitable excavation sites for most woodpeckers and thus no cavities for the secondary users. Meanwhile, the one woodpecker that can provide cavities in these pine forests will suffer intense eviction pressure from all the cavity competitors. This competition for the cavities which it alone can provide will reduce the reproductive success of the red-cockaded woodpecker, perhaps to extinction, at which point there will be neither cavities nor the means to provide them. All the services provided by the community of cavity-nesting animals, be it insect control, pollination, or seed dispersal, will disappear from the forest ecosystem.

We need to address one further aspect of red-cockaded woodpecker cavities: How do the cavity and its attendant resin wells affect the tree itself? Does the cavity weaken the structural integrity of the tree trunk? Do the numerous resin wells provide weak spots in a tree's defense mechanisms against pathogens? We have already disposed of the idea that resin wells facilitate entry and infection by pathogenic organisms. Indeed, the flow of resin is the tree's major defense against such infections at the site of injuries, such as insect borings and limb breakage. However, several observers have noted that pine trees occasionally break in half right at the level of the woodpecker cavity.

Red-cockaded woodpecker cavities typically measure about •
4 inches in diameter and 8 to 10 inches deep. The birds do
not excavate into the center of the tree before they begin to
deepen the cavity and create the roosting and nest chamber.
They seem to penetrate the tree just far enough to accommodate the chamber and then tunnel downward. When the
trunk is 11 to 20 inches in diameter at the height of the cavity,
as is typical, a 4-inch hole will not seriously weaken the tree. It
is not unusual to find larger trees that have two or more
cavities excavated at the same level. On rare occasions this
leads to a single cavity having two entrances. If the cavity is
constructed in a tree of small diameter, however, the cavity
will seriously weaken the tree. The smallest cavity tree I have
ever encountered was a mere 6½ inches in diameter at the
cavity, only 11 feet above the ground. The entrance tunnel
extended only 4 inches into the tree, and the bottom of the
cavity was 6 inches below the tunnel. This cavity also had a
vertical chamber 4 inches high above the tunnel, a rare feature, perhaps the result of such cramped quarters. When discovered, the cavity housed a flying squirrel. No competitor
had enlarged the entrance tunnel. Had this tree not been
protected by additional pines of similar size or larger in the
immediate vicinity, it would have probably broken in the
wind, for the walls of the cavity were barely an inch thick.

When larger woodpeckers appropriate cavities, they generally enlarge them. This is particularly true if the culprit is a
pileated woodpecker, and much of the trunk breakage found
occurs where this species has enlarged red-cockaded cavities
beyond safe limits. Since the red-cockaded woodpecker usually places its cavities just below the lowermost branches, the
entire crown of the tree breaks off and the tree dies. Thus,
while trees can generally tolerate the damage red-cockaded
woodpeckers inflict directly, subsequent damage from other
nest competitors can kill the tree providing the shelter.

In summary, the red-cockaded woodpecker excavates a
unique cavity below the crown in the main trunk, rather than

the upper extremities, of living pine trees. It uses the cavities for roosting the year round and for nesting during the spring and summer and prefers to excavate in wood softened by red heart fungus wherever possible. The woodpecker drills resin wells to cover the outside of the cavity tree with sticky pine resin, apparently as a deterrent to snakes. The cavities tend to face the west or southwest, an exposure which should facilitate the flow of resin. Many other species covet the cavities as valuable homes for themselves. While the cavity tree may suffer from the woodpecker activity, the forest as a whole benefits from the insect consumption and seed dispersal services that animals that use the red-cockaded woodpecker cavities provide.

The Generalist, the Specialist, and the Ecological Niche

No SPECIES, RARE or common, lives on its own, apart and disconnected from everything else in its environment. To discover why any given species goes extinct, we must examine how it fits into the surrounding community. In this chapter we will define the ecological niche of the red-cockaded woodpecker. We can define this niche only in the context of the red-cockaded woodpecker's connections to other woodpecker species in the bark-foraging guild. Is the red-cockaded woodpecker a generalist moderately efficient in exploiting a number of resources broadly distributed throughout its habitat? Or is it a specialist highly efficient in exploiting a few resources but inherently vulnerable to perturbations affecting these basic needs?

The concept of an ecological niche has developed into a basic tenet over the past 75 years. It is intellectually appealing, but almost impossible to define, much less measure. Much of the confusion arises from the intermingling of an organism's habitat and niche. We can draw a very simple analogy from human experience to explain the difference. The neighborhood in which you live and work is your habitat. It may consist of two distinct parts: where you sleep, eat, and rear your children and where you work. How you earn your living to support yourself, your family, and your dwelling is your niche. You may occupy a highly specialized niche that provides substantial income. If you lose your job (competition), or if your position is eliminated (job extinction), you may have to seek a less specialized position that provides less income. In doing so, you will likely have to shift your work habitat. If your new income cannot support your current dwelling, you may be forced to shift your home habitat as well. On the other hand, you may, through experience and education, be promoted or hired "upward" into a rarer, perhaps more specialized job. This rise may provide additional income and support an "upscale" move to new home and work habitats. Your niche correlates with your occupation, your habitat correlates with your address, at home and at work, and both occupation and address are highly intermingled. You may be highly specialized and limited in occupation and address or a broad generalist able to move freely among less skilled occupations, employers, and living quarters.

A woodpecker's habitat is typically a forest or open areas with scattered trees or tree surrogates, such as large cacti or utility poles. We define the niche of a woodpecker according to what it eats, how and where it obtains this food, and where it can construct cavities for shelter and reproduction—in other words, the basic necessities of life: food, shelter, and production of the succeeding generation. We assume that woodpeckers, like humans, will face competition for all these basic needs. Thus the habitat and niche which we observe for a given species may not be ideal. Certain desirable niche or habitat features may be absent or exist in short supply. Competitors may displace a species out of its optimal niche or habitat. We must therefore consider the difference between an animal's fundamental niche, defined in terms of its basic requirements and tolerance for environmental variability, and its realized niche, that which the animal can maintain in the face of competition from other species or other individuals of its own species. This distinction is particularly important when we consider endangered species with declining populations. How can we determine what is missing from the niche or in short supply if the ingredient is already gone or is rare in the environment?

We have considered the unique woodpecker home, its cavity, in the preceding chapter. We learned that the red-cockaded woodpecker is a highly specialized cavity builder and subsequently faces intense competition from other species for possession of these cavities. Let us now consider that primal necessity, food. When we study abundant species, it is straightforward, though not easy, to observe individuals of a species feeding, to collect an adequate number of the animals, and to analyze their stomach contents to determine what, and how many, food items the animal has eaten. This technique is not an option when we deal with endangered species. We must resort to indirect methods: observations of foraging birds or identification of food items brought to nestlings. Observations at the nest can help with large, readily identifiable prey, such as moths, but they fail when several prey items are jammed together in the adult's bill and impossible to distinguish.

An observer can determine where a woodpecker feeds by noting its behavior, but distinguishing what it eats is more difficult. When you check the tree a woodpecker feeds on, or one like it, you may observe nothing, or you may see several species of potential prey. Does the woodpecker eat all of them or any of them? Is it feeding on prey you have overlooked, or have the prey been removed before you looked? If you see the bird excavate prey by drilling, you can search similar pieces of bark, but you cannot be certain that what you observe tunneling in the tree is the subject of the woodpecker's hunt. So how are we to distinguish what an endangered species is feeding on, as opposed to more common woodpeckers? We can do it by comparing where the endangered species feed, and how they feed, with where and how the more common species feed.

Joe Skorupa and I conducted such a study on the Savannah River Plant, a 200,000-acre National Environmental Research Park operated by the U.S. Department of Energy in South Carolina. We compared the feeding ecology of the red-cockaded woodpecker with that of the numerous other woodpecker species by measuring where, and how, the birds foraged. We wanted to determine which, if any, of the other woodpeckers inhabiting these woodlands might compete with the red-cockaded woodpecker for food, perhaps to the point of contributing to the red-cockaded's rarity. These forests were a mixture of mature pines and hardwood trees. The pines grew to a typical height for the soil conditions and then slowly increased in girth as they aged. The trees all looked the same: The lower half of each tree was tall and slender, without branches, while the upper half formed a ovoid crown of trunk and branches. Many studies of birds' feeding habits have spent a great deal of effort measuring the height of foraging birds above the ground. In addition to the extra time required, this measurement is subject to error. We reasoned that the birds responded to the actual structure of the tree and did not care how high above the ground they were. So we recorded where in the tree the birds were foraging, which we could determine quickly and without measurement error. A bird foraged either on the trunk below the crown (below the lowest branch), on the trunk within the crown (above the lowest branch), on a primary limb (one attached directly to the trunk), on a secondary limb (a smaller limb attached to a larger primary limb), or on the ground. We also noted whether the tree was a pine, a hardwood species, a vine, or a fallen log and whether the bird foraged on living wood or deadwood. We recorded the sex of each bird studied, since other workers had noted differences in foraging habits between males and females. Finally, we studied the birds during the summer, when food would most likely be abundant, and again during the winter, when food might be scarce.

Until recently nine species of woodpeckers lived on the Savannah River Plant, making it the richest assemblage of woodpeckers in the world. Evidence still exists that the ivory-billed woodpecker, now apparently extinct, once inhabited these forests. Two of the eight species of woodpeckers that still live in these forests are migrants. The yellow-bellied sapsucker nests in more northerly areas but winters here every year. The red-headed woodpecker nests on the Savannah River Plant but spends the winter elsewhere. The northern flicker is a common resident year-round but frustrated our efforts to gather data about its foraging habits. A substantial ground cover—that is to say, herbaceous plants and woody saplings growing on the forest floor—thrives in these forests. We frequently flushed flickers from the ground but seldom were aware of their presence before they flew. We never observed a flicker foraging in the trees; that is not surprising since flickers are principally ground feeders. However, we can only infer that they were feeding before our approach flushed them. We surmised that the flicker is probably the most specialized in feeding habits of the entire group, but we cannot prove it.

We did gather data on the five other woodpecker species that permanently reside on the Savannah River Plant—the red-cockaded, downy, hairy, red-bellied, and pileated woodpeckers—plus the two migrants. We were able to determine the sex of each bird observed, with the exception of the pileated and red-headed woodpeckers. We frequently observed the large pileateds from distances too great to determine reliably the sex of the birds and had to combine all data for this species. The sex of red-headed woodpeckers cannot be determined by external appearance. The red-cockaded woodpeckers, whose sex is nearly impossible to distinguish in the field, we previously had captured, sexed, and marked with a unique combination of colored leg bands that permitted us to identify individual birds.

The differences in foraging habits between species, between sexes of the same species, and between seasons appear in Figure 5-1, pp. 120–21. The red-cockaded woodpecker almost always foraged on pine trees, rather than hardwood species, and rarely searched for prey on dead tree trunks or limbs. Males seldom foraged on lower trunks, particularly in winter. Females fed almost exclusively on trunks, seldom venturing onto limbs. Both sexes changed their habits very little from summer to winter. The downy woodpecker is closest in size to the red-cockaded but distinctly different in foraging habits. Downy females used pine trees substantially but males did not, particularly in winter. Both sexes foraged mostly on limbs, rather than trunks, especially in winter. The hairy woodpecker, which many bird watchers consider to be a larger version of the downy, has different foraging habits. Both sexes used pine trees far more in summer than in winter. Males shifted from dead pine in summer to live hardwood in winter. Females used live pine in summer but live hardwood in winter. Neither sex spent much time on secondary limbs. Yellow-bellied sapsuckers of both sexes spent 100 percent of their foraging efforts on live pine trunks. This is not surprising since they were winter migrants and we made the observations during January, when most hardwoods had neither foliage nor sap flow.

The larger, omnivorous red-bellied woodpecker is distinct both genetically and ecologically. Males spent 82 percent of their foraging in pines and 18 percent in hardwoods both summer and winter, mostly on trunks. Females shifted from foraging half the time on pines in summer to all the time on pines in winter, also primarily on trunks. Both sexes utilized deadwood but preferred live wood. Its close relative the red-headed woodpecker spent 60 percent foraging in pines, 12 percent in hardwoods, and 28 percent on the ground. These summer residents foraged on both live wood and deadwood everywhere within the trees. The largest woodpecker, the pileated, shifted from 90 percent of the time on pines in summer to 85 percent of the time on hardwoods in winter. This species alone was observed foraging on fallen logs, but only during the summer. Of summer sightings, 10 percent were on logs, verifying the common name of the pileated woodpecker in some regions of the country, the logcock.

Comparing the right and left halves of each column in the figure, we can see that both sexes of each species have a slightly different foraging microhabitat. This phenomenon is common among woodpeckers, and quite reasonable, for a bird's greatest competitor for scarce resources is most likely to be its own mate or offspring. Any tendency for the sexes to forage in a slightly different manner or in a different place will tend to reduce this competition. We speak of "ecological morphs" in this context, for each sex occupies a somewhat different niche in the habitat. I am certain that had we been able to distinguish the sexes of the pileated woodpeckers we observed, we would have seen a sexual difference in this species as well. Because of this sexual difference, we are able to speak not just of 7 different woodpecker species in the forest but of 12 ecological morphs: 2 sexual morphs for each of 5 species, plus the red-headed and pileated species. This characteristic seems so pervasive one may assume that it exists, unrecognized, in red-headed woodpeckers. It may also exist among the highly specialized flickers feeding on the ground.

We can use proportional foraging data of this nature to estimate the relative "breadth" of an ecological niche and then to calculate an index of relative specialization. That is,

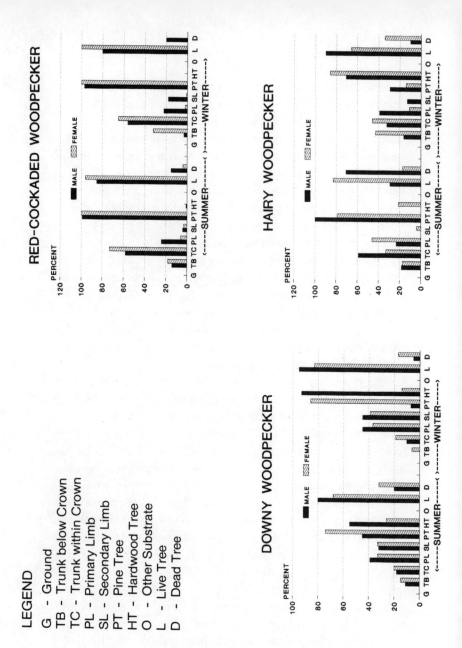

FIGURE 5-1 The foraging position and substrate favored by male and female woodpeckers during summer and winter.

RED-BELLIED WOODPECKER

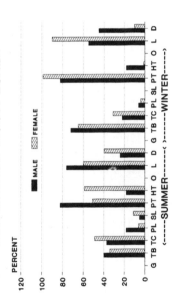

RED-HEADED WOODPECKER

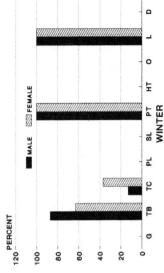

PILEATED WOODPECKER

YELLOW-BELLIED SAPSUCKER

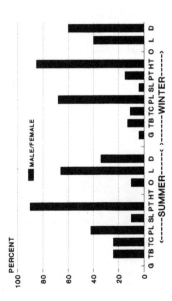

we can rank these ecomorphs from the most specialized to the most generalized. Specialists would have theoretically a very limited niche which they are able to exploit efficiently, while generalists would have a much broader niche, indicating their ability to shift their diet from one type of food to another as availability varies. We can also estimate how "plastic" a given niche may be by examining its structure during the summer, when food is abundant, and again in winter, when food resources may be more difficult to acquire. A single species might be able to feed solely on a given food source during the summer and to shift to a second, no less specialized source of food during the winter; but the food should be found in a different location, and we should be able to detect this foraging change.

The above discussion has focused on one aspect of a woodpecker's behavior: Where does the bird fly or climb to in its search for food? We can apply the same reasoning to a second behavioral trait: How does the woodpecker locate and capture its prey at that site?

The first technique which immediately comes to mind is the one that gave woodpeckers their name—the pecking of wood, or *percussion*. The bird slowly ascends a tree trunk, tapping the surface and occasionally drilling into the trunk to expose a gallery or tunnel beneath the surface. This form of hunting is the most conspicuous because an observer can detect an unseen bird by the sounds of the percussion. A more common technique is *search-and-probe*. The bird ascends the trunk, peering into the cracks and crevices of the bark, probing deeper with its bill, and capturing prey with its sticky tongue. *Scaling* is a more specialized technique, in which the bird inserts its bill into a crack or crevice and, with a flick of its head, causes a piece of bark to flake off, exposing animal prey hidden underneath. Large woodpeckers use a variation of this technique to separate large pieces of dead bark from the tree trunk, again exposing insect larvae and other prey. *Gleaning* involves foraging about the needles and leaves of the tree, picking leaf-eating insects or spiders from the foliage. *Sapsucking* is the highly specialized technique of excavating sap wells in the trunk and repeatedly visiting these wells to collect sap or insects attracted to the sap. Ants are a favorite prey of woodpeckers everywhere and commonly live on tree trunks and limbs. A few woodpeckers fancy ants so much that they leave the protection of the trees to forage directly on the ground, particularly at ant mounds, a behavior appropriately termed *anting*. A few woodpeckers resort to *fly-catching*, which involves sallying forth from a perch to capture a flying insect in midair.

Most woodpeckers utilize a combination of several of these techniques depending on the specific tree, habitat, or season they are foraging. As we can see in Figure 5-2, pp. 124–25. there are distinct differences in foraging technique between the sexes of a given species and between seasons of the year. All species use percussion, especially in winter. In summer male hairy woodpeckers use it most often, 35 percent of the time. In winter pileateds (79 percent), female hairy (71 percent), and male downy woodpeckers (54 percent) use percussion most frequently. Search-and-probe was the dominant foraging behavior during the summer for all species except the red-headed woodpecker. It remained the dominant behavior in winter for all ecomorphs except male downy, female hairy, and pileated woodpeckers and sapsuckers. Scaling was common with red-cockadeds, which flick off small pieces of pine bark at the surface, and pileateds, which strip whole pieces of dead bark away from tree trunks. Flycatching was most conspicuous in red-headed woodpeckers, but it was a small component of their repertoire. Gleaning occurred sporadically in a number of species and was a major component of red-headed woodpecker foraging. Only sapsuckers used sapsucking. About half the sapsucker observations were percussion; half, sapsucking. Since the tongue of the sapsucker lacks the spined, horny tip that would permit it to extract boring insect larvae, it may use percussion largely in

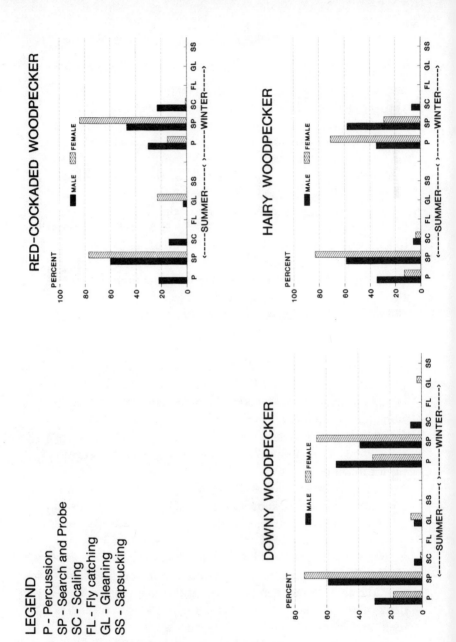

LEGEND
P - Percussion
SP - Search and Probe
SC - Scaling
FL - Fly catching
GL - Gleaning
SS - Sapsucking

FIGURE 5-2 The foraging behavior favored by male and female woodpeckers during summer and winter.

RED-BELLIED WOODPECKER

PERCENT

■ MALE   ▧ FEMALE

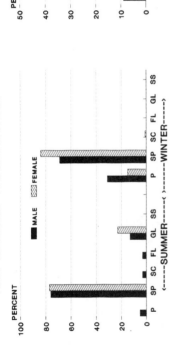

<-----SUMMER-----< >-----WINTER----->

P SP SC FL GL SS P SP SC FL GL SS

RED-HEADED WOODPECKER

PERCENT

■ MALE/FEMALE

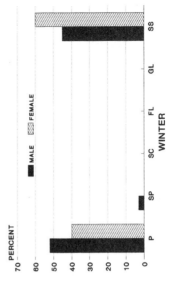

P   SP   SC   FL   GL   SS

SUMMER

PILEATED WOODPECKER

PERCENT

■ MALE/FEMALE

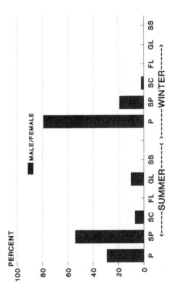

<-----SUMMER-----< >-----WINTER----->

P SP SC FL GL SS P SP SC FL GL SS

YELLOW-BELLIED SAPSUCKER

PERCENT

■ MALE   ▧ FEMALE

P   SP   SC   FL   GL   SS

WINTER

the formation and maintenance of sap wells. Only 3 percent, and then only male, of sapsucker foraging involved search-and-probe action.

Foraging behavior of the male hairy woodpeckers was remarkably constant: 35 percent percussion, 58 percent search-and-probe, and 6 percent gleaning in both summer and winter. This consistency seems even more remarkable when you consider that it involved a shift from 100 percent mostly dead pine tree foraging in summer to 71 percent mostly live hardwoods in winter. Females shifted from 83 percent search-and-probe in summer to 71 percent percussion in winter. Recall that this accompanies a shift from 79 percent pine trees in summer to 86 percent hardwood trees in winter. This ecomorph appears to occupy two totally distinct seasonal niches.

When we sum up the information about these three physical characteristics (position on live wood or deadwood in pine or hardwood tree) and about foraging behavior for both seasons, we have an estimate, a relative specialization index, of where and how a given woodpecker ecomorph searches for its food. When it is ranked along a scale from 0 to 1, we can compare whether an ecomorph is highly specialized (near the 0 end) or broadly generalized (approaching 1). We find (Figure 5-3, opposite) that the red-headed woodpeckers are the greatest generalists of the assemblage and that the yellow-bellied sapsuckers specialize the most. The red-headed woodpeckers use 5 of the 6 behaviors (see Figure 5-2) to capture prey (disdaining only sapsucking) and all the foraging locations (see Figure 5-1). No other woodpecker comes close to doing so many things in so many different places. The sapsuckers are at the other extreme. They drill holes, presumably to create sap wells, and suck sap (see Figure 5-2). We saw one sapsucker search and probe, probably eating ants. The sapsuckers forage only on the trunks of live pine trees (see Figure 5-1). It is interesting that the two extremes are the two migrant species. That the sapsucker is so specialized is almost expected, and its migratory habit is quite understandable.

That the most generalized red-headed woodpecker should also migrate is surprising.

Considering the five resident woodpeckers, we find a clumping of the pileated, downy, hairy, and red-bellied woodpecker ecomorphs midway along the scale (from 0.46 to 0.64). The male red-cockaded woodpecker is positioned in the middle of the group (0.55). The female red-cockaded (0.33) lies between the female (0.35) and male (0.32) sapsuckers as the most specialized of the assemblage. The female red-cockaded

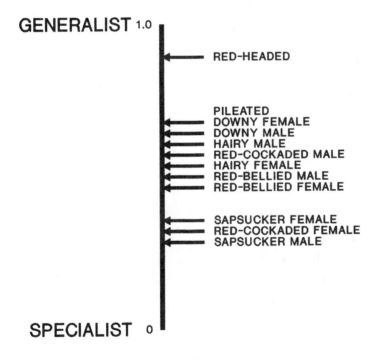

FIGURE 5-3 The relative specialization of woodpecker ecological morphs, ranging from the most generalized (red-headed woodpecker) to the most specialized (male yellow-bellied sapsucker).

is the most specialized of the woodpecker ecomorphs found in the forest throughout the year. Examining the seasonal variation exhibited in foraging sites (horizontal scale of Figure 5-1), we note that the red-cockadeds display the least variation between summer and winter sites. Pileated, both hairy, and the female red-bellied ecomorphs exhibit the greatest seasonal difference in where they forage.

What conclusions can we draw from this exercise? Clearly the differences in foraging locality and behavior between the two sexes of a given species can exceed the differences between species. The concept of distinct ecomorphs appears valid. The yellow-bellied sapsuckers are the most specialized in terms of foraging sites and behavior. An intriguing, but unanswered, question remains: Why do sapsuckers vacate the area during the summer? At the other extreme, the red-headed woodpeckers are the least specialized ecomorph during the summer, but they are unable to persist in this forest during the winter. Why?

The red-cockaded woodpeckers are highly specialized in terms of where they forage but not in how they forage. The two sexes occupy distinct niches but display very little shift between summer and winter. They "do their thing" in the same place and the same way all year round. A cluster of other woodpecker species tends to be equally generalized in their selection of foraging site, with large seasonal shifts, but they differ widely in the behavior they utilize to capture their prey at those sites.

We must next ask a critical question: How does this indirect estimation of what woodpeckers eat compare with actual stomach analyses? We are fortunate to have a substantial data base for comparison. In 1885 the U.S. Congress, in all its wisdom, appropriated funds to the Department of Agriculture for the study of "economic ornithology." One year later a Division of Economic Ornithology and Mammalogy was established within the Department of Agriculture to study the food habits, distribution, and migrations of birds and mammals and their relation to agriculture, horticulture, and forestry. A fruitful collaboration between entomologists and ornithologists persisted for a number of years as the scientists sought to discover which birds consumed both harmful and beneficial insects. One product was a report published in 1911 which described the stomach contents of 3,453 wood-peckers of 16 species collected from all parts of the United States. We will probably never see a study of this magnitude ever undertaken again.

A caveat or two is in order at this point. Every study in-troduces a certain amount of bias into the data produced. This bias may be from the particular questions being asked, the manner in which the data are collected, the design of the study, or it may simply be unavoidable. A scientist hopes to minimize these biases to the greatest extent possible. In lieu of that, one must be constantly aware of these inherent biases while interpreting the data. For example, in the foraging site and behavior study I have been describing I make no mention of any plant material being consumed by the woodpeckers. But harvesting of plant products by woodpeckers is a well-known phenomenon. This artifact in our study may have resulted from the seasons during which data were collected: early to midsummer and again in early winter. Fruits and acorns are typically most abundant during late summer and autumn. We collected no data on the occurrence or abun-dance of fruits or mast (acorns or other nuts) in the forest. Every study has time or funding limitations, and questions regarding the identification and abundance of any food source were beyond the scope of our study; but we must re-member and recognize the problem of inherent biases.

The second caveat involves determining food habits by analysis of stomach contents. Not all animal or plant parts are equally digestible. Therefore, they do not remain as identifi-able fragments in the stomach for equal periods of time fol-lowing ingestion. For example, many birds eagerly eat the fruit of poison ivy. The birds digest the pulp tissue of the berry at a moderate rate, and it soon becomes unidentifiable and difficult to differentiate from other fruits or berries. The seeds, however, resist digestion and pass from the birds' digestive tract unharmed. The seeds remain recognizable in the stomach and intestines for hours. The same is true of insects. Hard-bodied beetles persist as recognizable particles for a fairly long time. Birds quickly digest soft-bodied caterpillars or insect larvae, which may be unrecognizable as soon as five minutes after ingestion. The hard, chitinous mouthparts may lodge in the stomach and persist for a day or two. Similarly, acorn meat will persist much longer than soft berries. A foodstuff such as tree sap may be totally undetectable. Thus, when you open a stomach, you may find a caterpillar just consumed, a berry eaten an hour or two before, grasshopper mandibles that may have been around since the day before, and amorphous "yuck" of unknown origin and longevity. Next, you must estimate the relative volume of this food and relative proportion of the total diet which these items represent. The numbers produced give an impression of "hard data," but the amount of confidence we can be place in them is small. Nevertheless, the numbers do tell us something, for such remains are the only real evidence that a food item was actually consumed, so let us proceed.

The 1911 report written by F. E. L. Beal classified the stomach contents as either animal or vegetable matter and identified the major components in each category. The animal fraction ranged from as high as 94 percent in the highly arboreal three-toed woodpecker to a low of 23 percent in the appropriately named acorn woodpecker. Within our South Carolina assemblage of 9 species, the animal fraction ranged from a high of 81 percent for the red-cockaded woodpecker down to 31 percent for the red-bellied woodpecker. Keep in mind that the study collected these data from 33 states, and the numbers do not verify what these species would eat in South Carolina. For example, the red-cockaded woodpeckers came from Florida, Alabama, Louisiana, and Texas. Sample sizes are also very important and generally were more than adequate. The smallest samples represented were 76 red-cockaded woodpeckers and 80 pileated woodpeckers. Other species were more abundant in the study: 382 hairy, 723 downy, 443 red-headed and 271 red-bellied woodpeckers, 684 flickers, and 313 yellow-bellied sapsuckers. Such numbers may be repugnant to contemporary readers, but they are as essential to good science today as they were at the turn of the century.

The staple of the woodpecker diet is undoubtedly ants. All species consumed ants, sometimes in prodigious numbers. The stomach of one flicker contained more than 5,000. Ants constituted 28 percent of all food consumed by all 16 woodpecker species nationwide. Within our 9-species woodpecker assemblage, ants formed 56 percent of the animal prey consumed by red-cockaded woodpeckers and 50 percent consumed by flickers (see Table 5) but only 5 and 6 percent for red-headed and red-bellied woodpeckers respectively. While we would expect the ground-feeding flickers to be major ant consumers, it comes as quite a surprise to learn that red-cockaded woodpeckers consumed even more. The 2 species do not compete for ants, for the red-cockaded concentrates

WOODPECKER DIETS

Species	Number	Percent Vegetable Food	Percent Animal Food	Percent of Animal Food as	
				Ants	Beetles
Red-Cockaded	76	19	81	56	11
Downy	723	24	76	21	22
Hairy	382	22	78	17	11
Sapsucker	313	51	49	34	6
Flicker	684	39	61	50	5
Red-Bellied	271	69	31	6	10
Red-Headed	443	66	34	5	19
Pileated	80	17	73	40	22

on arboreal ants while the flicker preys on terrestrial species.

Figure 5-4 plots the percentage of the diet composed of animal matter on the horizontal axis against the percentage of ants in this animal matter on the vertical axis. The results demonstrate once again that these woodpeckers occupy different niches. Even the close pairs are not as close as they seem. The red-bellied and red-headed woodpeckers may consume similar dietary proportions of mast, fruits, and beetles, but the red-bellied plies its trade in the forest and rarely stores acorns or other foodstuffs. The red-headed woodpecker pre-

ANTS AND ANIMALS IN WOODPECKER DIETS

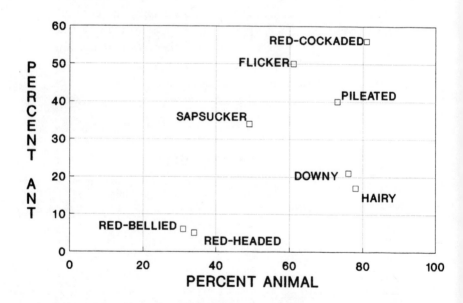

FIGURE 5-4 The dietary niche of woodpeckers, ranging from the predominantly vegetarian red-bellied and red-headed woodpeckers who eat few ants, to the highly insectivorus red-cockaded woodpeckers who eat the most ants.

fers more open forest, indulges in some flycatching of insects in midair, and is an inveterate hoarder of acorns and other mast. In the Midwest this species may remain all winter or migrate elsewhere, depending upon the success of the acorn crop that fall. Perhaps acorns are the key to the winter migration away from the Savannah River Plant, for elsewhere in South Carolina the red-headed woodpecker may overwinter. Similarly, the downy and hairy woodpeckers seem close together, but the downy's prey includes beetles, ants, and caterpillars, while the hairy exploits more wood-boring beetle larvae. Pileateds concentrate on large wood-boring ants and beetle larvae. Surprises include sapsuckers' consuming 49 percent animal matter, 34 percent of its being ants. Is this a distortion caused by a poor ability to detect tree sap in stomach samples?

All in all, this "ancient" study, published in preliminary form in 1895, and final form in 1911, illustrates one of my favorite scientific maxims: Good theories come and go, but good data last forever! While we might have predicted the flicker to be the anteater nonpareil, the red-cockaded woodpecker seems to be a strong contender, if not actual champion, in this arena, and the sapsucker is no slacker as a formicivore. Likewise, neither our subjective observations nor our niche estimators would have anticipated that two-thirds of the diet of red-headed and red-bellied woodpeckers would be plant material. This study even gives us a glimpse of what the now-extinct ivory-billed woodpeckers were eating. Only two of these stomachs were examined, but they contained 38 percent large wood-boring beetle larvae, plus magnolia fruits and pecans.

We can now compare how the 9 species of woodpeckers in this southeastern assemblage resemble one another and explore how their similarities and differences illuminate their evolutionary history. We can call all of them omnivores because they all consume both plant and animal matter, though there are distinct differences in the ratio of animal to plant material, where they search for their food, and the manner in which they capture it. There is 1 *Colaptes* species, the flicker, which is a ground woodpecker and forages on ants and various wild fruits. There are 2 *Centurus* species, the red-headed and red-bellied woodpeckers, that distinctly lean toward the herbivorous end of the dietary scale, both consuming mast, fruits, beetles, and a few ants. The red-bellied woodpeckers forage only in trees, in a general way, and shift their habits somewhat in the winter. The red-headed woodpeckers spend a fourth of their time foraging on the ground and equal time gleaning prey along the branches. They covet and store acorns and other nuts for later consumption and migrate elsewhere during the winter when insects, and perhaps mast, are scarce.

There is a single species of *Sphyrapicus*, the highly specialized yellow-bellied sapsucker, which only winters in the area, consuming sap, cambium, and ants. There is a single species of *Dryocopus*, the large pileated woodpecker, which peels bark and excavates in large trees to expose wood-boring beetle larvae and carpenter ants. The now-extinct *Campephilus*, the ivory-billed woodpecker, also scaled bark from large trees to feed on large beetle larvae and consumed fruit as well.

There are 3 *Picoides* species, all highly arboreal and insectivorous. The diminutive downy woodpecker concentrates on tree limbs, feeding on beetles, ants, and caterpillars. The larger hairy woodpecker concentrates on tree trunks and excavates a larger number of wood-boring larvae. The intermediate-size red-cockaded woodpecker concentrates on pine trees, scales small pieces of bark off tree trunks to expose animal prey, and feeds on large quantities of ants. Among the 3, the red-cockaded is the most specialized in its foraging sites and behavior. Strict limits govern where it forages and how it forages in both summer and winter.

We see that these woodpeckers have thriven because they each specialize in different resources within their common habitat. They have carved out individual niches not only among the different species but also between the two sexes of the same species. We have demonstrated that a minimum of 12 ecological niches for woodpeckers exist in this forest. Probably 18 niches formerly existed and 16 still do—2 for each of the species found here. The niches currently filled by the sapsuckers and the red-headed woodpeckers may be only seasonal, causing each to migrate elsewhere for part of the year. Some crucial aspect of the niche (niches?) formerly occupied by the ivory-billed woodpecker has disappeared or been reduced below a critical threshold. Likewise, some critical factor is diminishing for the red-cockaded woodpeckers here, for they have disappeared before our very eyes as we watched— helpless and ignorant, questioning, but not getting the right answers. We are clearly not asking the right questions to entice nature to reveal its secrets.

A Cooperative Nature

ONE OF THE most intriguing recent discoveries in biology has been the gradual realization that many breeding birds get help raising their young from other, nonbreeding individuals. We call this method of reproduction, which more than 200 species practice, cooperative breeding, and we call the birds themselves cooperative breeders.

Cooperative breeding occurs in several different forms. In the most common form one or more "helpers" assist the breeding pair raise their young by incubating the eggs, or brooding or feeding the nestlings, or feeding the fledglings. But only one male inseminates the female and only one female lays eggs in the nest. A second, less common type of cooperative breeding occurs when more than two birds participate in the production of the fertile eggs. This can involve two or more males and one female, who produce a single clutch of eggs, presumably fertilized in part by both males. It can also involve two or more females, mated to two or more males, who lay their eggs in a single nest and jointly raise the young. A third type occurs when two or more males display their plumage and vocal virtuosity in adjacent arenas to attract females, who, after copulation, go off to nest and raise their young independent of assistance from either their mate, or mates, or other females. In this instance some subordinate males helped attract females to the display ground but, depending on the whim of the females, were not chosen to contribute genes to the next generation.

Biologists use three criteria to determine which species are cooperative breeders. Three or more birds must help produce the eggs or care for the young, the offspring must come from a single nest, and a significant amount of cooperation must occur among the birds in the group. Considerable debate has arisen over this apparently altruistic behavior. Why would an individual capable of breeding forgo reproduction in order to assist other birds in raising their young? The nonbreeder would appear to act against its best interests. Why should one bird pass up an opportunity to contribute its own genes to the next generation but help some other bird to ensure persistence of the species?

Ornithologists were slow to discover that red-cockaded woodpeckers breed cooperatively. In 1939 E. E. Murphey wrote an account of this species in A. C. Bent's *Life Histories of North American Woodpeckers,* one volume in Bent's monumental series on North American birds. Murphey noted that the bird was quite gregarious, often lived in groups of 6 to 10 individuals, and built its nests in detached communities during the breeding season.

David Ligon was the first to note, in 1970, that some birds in a group were helpers. He discovered helpers by placing numbered aluminum leg bands and colored plastic bands in different combinations on the legs of adults and nestlings. Unique color band combinations enabled him to identify individual birds and study family intrarelationships within woodpecker clans. Two of the six clans Ligon observed in Florida had helpers, and one of these helpers he knew to be a male offspring from the previous year. Dan Lay, in Texas, and Wilson Baker, elsewhere in Florida, also noted the presence of helpers. Once they were discovered, everyone started looking for, and finding, helpers wherever red-cockaded woodpeckers lived. Biologists soon recognized that the role of helpers in brooding and feeding nestlings, feeding fledglings, and defending the territories was the rule, rather than an exception. A simple technique had led to a significant revelation. The right question had been asked: What are these extra birds so frequently seen in this gregarious species?

To the human eye, individual woodpeckers are difficult to tell apart. We might manage to distinguish among individuals through intensive study of a handful of birds. But biologists seek generalizations that apply to all or most individuals, not the quirks of a mere handful. It is nearly impossible for a biologist to learn the individual characteristics of more than a few birds, particularly when each bird molts its entire plumage once a year, shedding its recognized feather pattern.

Inexpensive color bands solved that problem. With binoculars, good light, and a dash of good luck, a patient biologist can identify a specific bird not seen for months or years. Soon after Ligon's study, a new kind of hunter began stalking the pineywoods. Instead of carrying a large rifle with a small telescope perched on top, this hunter carried a telescope "gun." He or she shouldered a rifle stock equipped with a spotting telescope and took careful aim into the treetops, but no rifle shot disturbed the woods. At most, you might have heard a "gotcha" as a woodpecker watcher deciphered the color band combination and quickly entered it into a field notebook.

Fishing in the treetops also became popular. Biologists cast nylon nooses into cavities, gently eased nestlings into the bright light of the outside world, and adorned them with colored anklets. Researchers were able to sex, age, and identify woodpeckers as never before. Fascinating patterns began to emerge. When a single woodpecker was found at a cluster of cavity trees, it was invariably a male. If two birds were present, it was a mated pair, male and female. When more than two birds were present, the extra bird or birds were almost invariably male and usually the offspring from a previous year.

We discovered that red-cockaded woodpeckers hatched and raised equal numbers of male and female nestlings, but the two sexes did not enjoy an equal opportunity for survival. Some male offspring left the clan, while others remained to become helpers. But virtually no female offspring were permitted, or chose, to remain. They disappeared from their natal group at some time between fall and spring. Frequently they simply disappeared altogether.

Clearly the cavity trees and a surrounding exclusive territory were the keys to success for these woodpeckers. A male that had a cavity and a territory could attract a female, and the pair could become breeders. Males without territories could not secure mates. Males could remain with their parents as helpers, aiding in the defense of the territory and the raising of their siblings. If the territorial breeding male died, his son could inherit the territory. Both males and females could become floaters, unattached to clans and without territories. A female that found a male without a mate could become a breeder. In a sense, a three-class society existed: breeders, attended by helpers, surrounded by floaters.

Researchers became fascinated with this society of cooperative breeders. How did such a system evolve? What are the advantages and disadvantages of becoming a helper as opposed to a floater? What happens to the females? It quickly became clear that unraveling this mystery would require a massive effort over a lengthy period. Two North Carolina State University biologists, Phil Doerr and Jay Carter, took up the challenge, later joined by Jeff Walters and a bevy of graduate and undergraduate students. They formed a cooperative research group to study this cooperative breeder. They set out to capture, band, and study all the birds in a given population. The cornucopia of information now emerging, six years and 500 banded woodpeckers later, is vivid testimony to their success and to the foresight of their funding agencies.

The strategy of the NCSU group has been deceptively simple: Band every bird present or born into the population and track what happens to each one, to determine who mates with whom, and how long they live in the area. The researchers have been so successful that the sudden appearance of an unbanded bird in their midst is a personal affront, which they pursue relentlessly until it becomes a marked bird. Their diligence has paid off, immensely enriching our knowledge of this species.

The fate of breeding males, the top of the hierarchy, is shown in Figure 6-1, opposite. From one year to the next, 71 percent will remain as breeders, but 24 percent will simply disappear, assumed to have died from some natural cause. In addition, 2 percent will become solitary males, principally because of the loss of breeding females without a replacement, while 3 percent will abandon their territories and move elsewhere. This is apparently a wise strategy because two-thirds of the birds that move become breeders somewhere else. However, 24 percent establish other territories without successfully attracting mates, and 12 percent simply become floaters. Some of these floaters may be old males that have been displaced by younger, more vigorous males, perhaps even their own offspring.

The fate of male helpers is shown in Figure 6-2, p. 142. Fully half the helpers remain as helpers the following year, while 20 percent disappear and are presumed dead. But 17

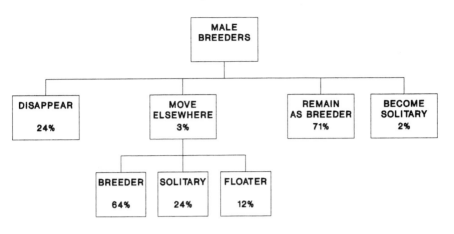

FIGURE 6-1 The fate of breeding male red-cockaded woodpeckers.

percent inherit territories, typically their natal territories, as the breeding males disappear. Of these sons that inherit the territories, 90 percent become breeders. Some 13 percent of helper males disperse to other territories, and 91 percent of these males become breeders. Typically they disperse to adjacent territories that become available when the territorial males disappear. Thus 30 percent of the helper males either inherit the territories of the males they are assisting or acquire neighboring territories. Accepting a subservient role as a helper for a year or so is definitely a viable strategy for acquiring a territory and becoming a breeding male.

Solitary males arise in two ways. First, they may be dispersing males that locate abandoned cavity trees and establish territories in hopes of attracting females. Second, they may have formerly bred on their territories but subsequently have lost their mates. The fate of solitary males is shown in Figure 6-3, p. 143, which points out that 18 percent fail to attract females and remain solitary males, while 38 percent simply disappear. But 26 percent succeed in attracting mates and become breeders. Some 18 percent move elsewhere, and 81

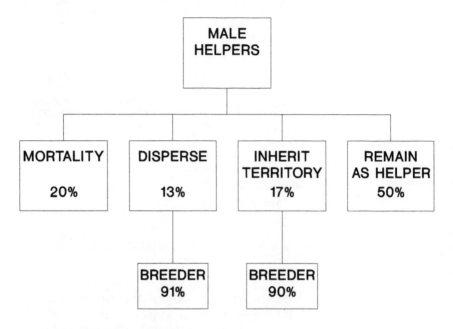

FIGURE 6-2 The fate of helper male red-cockaded woodpeckers.

percent of these males that relocate become breeders.

Adult female birds, which do not establish territories of their own, show a different pattern (Figure 6-4, opposite). More than half (56 percent) are still on the territories of their mates the following year. One-third simply disappear, 12 percent change territories to mate with other males, while 1 percent become floaters unattached to a territory.

What happens to the young of each year, those inexperienced juveniles trying to cope with the world and establish themselves within the social hierarchy? Distinct sexual discrimination appears to rule. Males have the most options (Figure 6-5, p. 144). A majority (57 percent) simply disappear, but a fourth (27 percent) remain on their natal territories to become helpers. A few males (3 percent) even inherit their fathers' territories upon the fathers' demise in their first year.

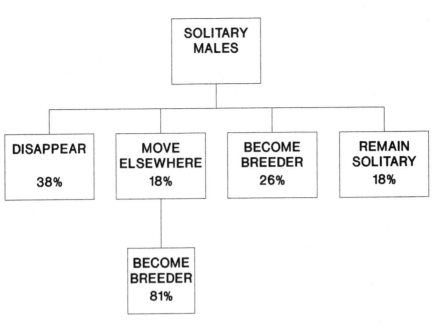

FIGURE 6-3 The fate of solitary male red-cockaded woodpeckers.

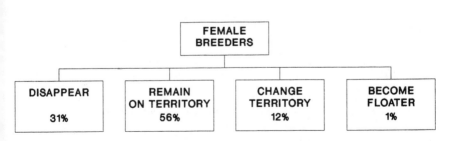

FIGURE 6-4 The fate of breeding female red-cockaded woodpeckers.

Three-fourths of these new landholders will successfully mate, but 25 percent of them inherit territories only to become solitary males. More on this phenomenon later. Only 13 percent of the young males that leave the nest actually disperse away from their territories. Many (70 percent) actually acquire territories although 39 percent will successfully breed while 31 percent become solitary males. A fourth become floaters, acquiring neither land nor mate, while 5 percent will become attached to other clans and become helpers to unrelated birds.

Female fledglings have fewer options (Figure 6-6, opposite). More than two-thirds (68 percent) simply disappear. A mere 1 percent remain on their natal territories, where 43 percent become breeders and 57 percent become helpers. Nearly a third of the females disperse away from the natal territory, in what appears to be a good strategy because 92 percent become breeders, 6 percent float, and 1 percent become helpers to other clans.

How far do these woodpeckers disperse? Females can move considerable distances. Half the female fledglings moved farther than 2 miles, the farthest being 20 miles. But 29 percent

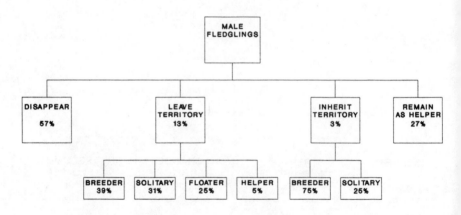

FIGURE 6-5 The fate of fledgling male red-cockaded woodpeckers.

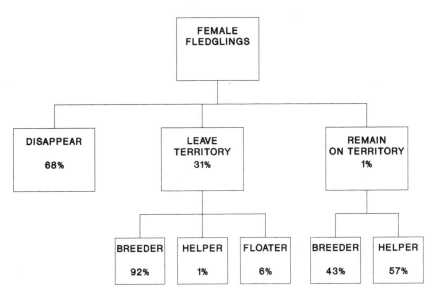

FIGURE 6-6 The fate of fledgling female red-cockaded woodpeckers.

moved no farther than the adjacent territory, and only 24 percent moved farther than 3 territories distant. In contrast, adult females that moved usually went less than 1 mile, with the farthest distance traveled being 9 miles. In fact, 61 percent of the adult females moved only to neighboring territories, and only 8 percent moved farther than 2 occupied territories away.

Males were less peripatetic. Only half the fledgling males went more than 3 miles, with a maximum of 13 miles. Adult males were even less inclined to travel, typically less than 1 mile, with a maximum 5 miles. Breeding males moved only to nearby colonies, but solitary males tended to move farther.

Dispersal of juveniles is understandable and occurs with most bird species. But why do adult birds move? In all instances when a breeding male moved, his female mate had died or left before him, leaving him as a solitary male. In no instance did a breeding male abandon a mate, a helper, or offspring. However, at least twice a breeder became a floater after being displaced by a new male.

The movement of breeding females is the most fascinating of all. The red-cockaded woodpecker is a territorial permanent resident of these forests, and young males may persist on natal territories to become helpers. These conditions are ripe for inbreeding, which invariably has negative effects as the result of an increase of deleterious genes in the population. Females appear to go to great lengths to avoid incestuous matings. When the dominant or breeding male dies, and a helper male is present in the group, the helper inherits the territory. If the helper is unrelated to the female, she may stay on the territory. But if the female is, in fact, the mother of the helper, she leaves and moves to a new group. If no helper is present when the breeding male dies, either an immigrant male moves onto the territory and mates with the female or she moves to another group. If the breeding female dies, a juvenile female will not remain to mate with her father, but she will remain if an unrelated male becomes the territory holder.

The function of floaters is now clear. They remain available, constantly roving the forest, ready to replace territorial birds when they die. Floaters are common in most bird species. They are frequently tolerated on the territories of other woodpeckers because they do not represent a threat, inasmuch as they are not attempting to take over and defend territories. They are just searching for unused cavities and unoccupied territories.

Male fledglings employ two distinct strategies. They can disperse and take their chances in the world beyond, or they can stay at home and become helpers. Which choice is the most rewarding? The choice seems permanent. No fledgling male observed farther away than an adjacent territory was ever known to return to his natal group. Few helpers become floaters. Does either strategy offer an advantage over the other?

Consider a scenario based on Figure 6-5 to forecast the fate of 100 male fledglings born into the population. Only 3 lucky birds will inherit their fathers' territories while 57 less fortunate birds fail to survive their first year. Only 13 bold fledglings will leave home. Of these 13, 4 will acquire territories but not mates during their first breeding season and thus contribute no offspring as solitary males. Of the 13, 5 will acquire both territories and mates and potentially contribute offspring to the population. Using the alternate strategy, 27 timid birds will remain at home as helpers and neither acquire territories nor contribute offspring to the population during their first year of reproductive potential.

As the birds enter their second breeding season, their lives continue to change. About 71 percent of the breeders will breed again (Figure 6-1). Some of the solitary birds will acquire mates while others move elsewhere, perhaps acquiring mates en route (Figure 6-3). Some floaters will acquire territories and mates. But disappearing birds and other losses keep the number of breeding males steady at 5.

Meanwhile, the 27 helpers change status as well (Figure 6-3). Some inherit territories, with or without mates. Some disperse to nearby territories and become breeders. Overall, 7.4 of the timid birds (27 percent of 27) will breed in their second year, while 5.2 of the bold birds (40 percent of 13) will do likewise. But this is the second time the bold birds have reproduced while it is only the first experience for the timid males. If we assume that each pair of woodpeckers fledges a pair of offspring, exactly reproducing themselves, the bold males will have produced 10.3 offspring in two years while twice as many timid males have sired only 7.4 birds. In terms of contribution to the woodpecker population, audacity appears to pay.

But as so often happens, our basic assumption is suspect.

Experience pays rich dividends in raising birds. The number of young birds successfully fledged from a nest almost always rises as the parents grow older. Two-year-old birds produce twice as many fledglings as one-year-old birds, and each additional year of experience, up to six years, continues to improve reproductive efficiency. Why should this be?

Young males have a particularly hard time. Only 16 percent of male birds acquire both territories and mates by the time they are one year old, but 69 percent of males will have acquired both territories and mates by the time they are three years old. As a result, helpers, solitary birds, and floaters are predominantly young males. Territorial pairs that include a one-year-old male often (36 percent) fail to nest, and those that do nest suffer a high rate (34 percent) of nest failure. One-year-old males virtually never have helpers at the nest, since most helpers are the male offspring of previous nesting. In light of this differential, age-related reproductive success, it may not be very costly for helpers to abstain from breeding for one or more years. They gain valuable experience in capturing prey, learning the location of food resources within the territory, defending the territory, evading predators, brooding nestlings, and feeding young birds.

Male red-cockaded woodpeckers thus pursue simultaneously two life strategies. Bolder males strike out on their own before they are one year old. They have the greatest chance to discover unoccupied territories, but these may be located in low-quality habitats. Should they enter pinewoods that lack suitable cavities, they will have no shelter until they can construct new cavities, a very lengthy process. Meanwhile, they may suffer from predation and the vagaries of weather. If they stray too far, they may not be found by dispersing females. If they mate, they may fail to nest or produce few offspring.

Alternatively males may elect not to leave their natal territories during their first year of life. Life may be easier for these males. They share territorial defense duties but are not solely responsible for them. They may utilize existing vacant cavities for shelter. They benefit from group detection of predators. They can make frequent excursions into neighboring territories to determine if they are still defended or contain breeding males. As males in adjacent territories disappear, the helpers will have first opportunity to replace them or take over vacated territories. Adjacent territories may be in higher-quality habitats than more distant, unoccupied space. Procrastination, remaining on their natal territories for one or more years until opportunity knocks, is a viable strategy. Since their reproductive potential will increase with age, postponing nesting may not reduce the lifetime reproductive output of these birds.

Adoption of the helper strategy benefits the helper. Does it also benefit the breeders? It is easy to imagine both benefits and drawbacks. Assume that resources, whether food or cavities, are limited. Inadequate food may lessen, or even prevent altogether, egg production by the female. Barely adequate food may allow nesting but limit nesting success. Abundant food may permit all nestlings to fledge. Successful nesting produces helpers, but can the territory support the breeding pair, the helpers, and additional offspring the following year? Groups with helpers appear to produce 0.6 more offspring than groups without helpers. There are so many confounding factors, however, such as the number of helpers, the age of the breeding pair, relationships between breeders and helpers, the number of cavities, food availability, and so on, that the helpers' actual effect is difficult to discern.

The effects of sexual discrimination are more obvious. Females rarely become helpers; thus they all disperse, although whether they do so by choice or by necessity is unknown. In two small coastal populations in North Carolina females have been found to constitute 18 percent and 21 percent of the helper population. A larger fraction of both males (37 percent) and females (10 percent) remains as helpers for their first year of life. The determining factor appears to be fierce competition for breeding territories in limited habitat.

Females suffer higher first-year mortality (68 percent versus 57 percent for males). Females do not inherit territories, even when helpers are not present at the time the breeding males disappear. New males become the landholders, and the females may have to vacate the premises. When the breeding male is succeeded by one of his sons, and the female is the mother of the helper male, the female, not the son, moves on.

Females are subordinate to males in all endeavors, even foraging. This can have unexpected effects. Jerry Jackson has noted that hardwood trees encroaching on the lower pine trunks on which females foraged forced the females higher into the trees, where they had to complete directly with the males. The females soon suffered, on the average, a 14 percent weight loss while males held their body weights steady. A weight loss of this magnitude can severely hinder reproductive success.

Two of the most common signs of declining populations are abandoned colonies and single-male colonies. Although single-male colonies can arise with an expanding population, as surplus one-year-old males disperse, these birds should eventually be discovered by dispersing females. In declining populations, single-male colonies arise as breeding females die without replacement by new birds. The augmentation of single males with immature females, transported from stable populations, is a promising tactic for rebuilding decimated populations.

There are many questions we must address before we can understand the evolution of a complex social system of this nature. Overall, there are four basic questions—why delay dispersal? why live in groups? why delay breeding? why help?—which are closely intertwined.

Tracing these questions through the course of a bird's life will help us get some answers. Both male and female fledglings of many species of birds stay with their parents for an extended period after birth. Dispersal can begin in late summer or early fall or even wait until early spring, but normally juvenile birds disperse before the new breeding season begins, either voluntarily or because they are evicted by the parents. The first year of life poses extreme hazards for all young birds, and dispersal is one of the most dangerous. The juveniles are on their own, no longer able simply to follow the lead of their parents, and living in unknown terrain, where they are unfamiliar with food sources, predators, escape routes, and safe havens.

In North Carolina 68 percent of female red-cockaded woodpecker fledglings simply disappeared, fate unknown, in their first year of life (see Figure 6-6). The researchers spotted only 31 percent of female fledglings elsewhere, but 92 percent of these birds successfully located mates with territories. So of 100 females fledged, 31 survived and 29 nested. Young females are very adept at locating territory-holding mates and reproducing.

Female red-cockaded woodpeckers do not delay dispersal or breeding. Male fledglings follow a different path early in their lives. Fewer (57 percent) disappear, but fewer disperse also (Figure 6-5). Out of 100 male fledglings, only 12 will inherit or locate territories, and only 7 of these will acquire mates and nest. Four times more females than males nest in their first year. More than a quarter (27 percent) of the year's production of males elect to delay dispersal and remain as helpers. The males are physiologically capable of breeding, but many lack the two necessary ingredients: a territory and a mate. There appears to be a shortage of both territories and females. Most juvenile males that survive their first winter choose to delay dispersal and breeding to remain at home.

Recall the first question: Why delay dispersal? A popular hypothesis credits habitat saturation, an ecological constraint. This view holds that some environmental factor, usually a shortage of space, constrains the dispersion of young birds, forcing them to remain with their natal groups. Thus, in staying at home, nonbreeding helpers are making the best of a bad situation and would breed on their own if they were able to find suitable territories.

Does our evidence support this view? The woodpeckers appear to compete for existing territories rather than create new ones. It seems to be very difficult for young males to disperse to brand-new stands of seemingly suitable pines, excavate new cavities, defend territories and attract mates. Red-cockaded woodpeckers usually create new cavities in existing colonies. Territories expand and contract. Clans disappear. New unions form, and the birds redistribute territories; but new colonies seem to appear only when existing cavity trees are reapportioned into new clusters. Thus cavities and clusters of cavity trees seem to act as a limiting factor. Once acquired, breeding males are faithful to their colony sites. Solitary males, if unable to attract females, are more likely to move to a different cluster of cavity trees. Breeding females are much more likely to "divorce" their mates or otherwise switch clans.

On the other hand, the presence of abandoned territories, a common feature among declining populations, argues against the habitat saturation hypothesis. The difficulty lies in determining why the birds have abandoned the colonies. Are they no longer suitable habitats? Have the existing cavities been rendered useless by cavity enlargement or hardwood encroachment? Is abandonment the result of population decline, attributable to reduced reproductive success or increased mortality?

Recall the second question: Why live in groups? We can easily imagine the benefits that come from group living. The birds travel and forage together. Young birds gain valuable experience by following and mimicking older birds. A larger group may be able to defend successfully a larger territory for its exclusive use, thereby retaining more resources as well. Inexperienced birds watch their parents raise siblings, learning by observation. But what causes helpers to participate?

A dispersing male, unable to acquire a territory that will attract a female, has few choices. He can roam in search of a territory and mate indefinitely or try to share a female with another male. There is no evidence of mate sharing (polyandry) in red-cockaded woodpeckers. Some juveniles, about 3 percent, do choose to roam as floaters. But 63 percent of one-year-old males remain on their natal territories as subordinate, nonbreeding helpers. There are two related questions here. Why do the males not disperse? A male certainly cannot find a territory unless he searches for one. But perhaps more important, why do the breeding males tolerate the continued presence of their sons?

We do not know why breeding males tolerate the continued presence of their sons. No researcher has formulated the right questions that will unlock this mystery. We can only surmise that considering limited territories and a shortage of females, the best strategy for a young male is to remain at home, in the company of his parents, and use the natal territory as a base from which to make short dispersal forays until he locates a vacant territory. It is easy to suggest that a breeding male would be more likely to tolerate his own offspring than a strange bird on the territory for an extended period. The benefits to the offspring are obvious: a familiar territory, parents as role models, guaranteed quality habitat, and so forth. The benefit to the breeders is less obvious and difficult to establish. The shortage of females provides a surplus of males, and tolerance of the parents leads to group living. Proving this scenario is still beyond us.

The answer to the third question—why delay breeding?—is more apparent. The shortage of females and territories makes delayed reproduction a viable strategy. Remaining on the natal territory is less risky than dispersal into the unknown. And the lifetime reproductive potential of the male that helps for one or more years before breeding may not be significantly less than that of the juvenile male that disperses during his first year.

The fourth question—why help?—is the toughest to resolve. A male that lingers on the natal territory gains all the benefits mentioned above without helping. Helping is something of a paradox. Helpers exhibit parental behavior (brooding and feeding young) although they are not the genetic parents of the nestlings and fledglings that benefit from their help. They undoubtedly gain useful experience. Does their helping behavior foster acceptance by the breeders? Do all extra birds actually help? How does a helper directly benefit by expending energy to raise its siblings rather than its own offspring? These questions await resolution.

Researchers have suggested hypotheses that explain why males delay dispersal and breeding other than habitat saturation. One may be called the skill hypothesis since it infers that young cooperative breeders have not acquired the skill necessary to breed independently and therefore delay breeding to remain with their natal groups until they gain sufficient skill. There is no doubt that experience leads to more successful reproduction in many, perhaps all species of birds and other animals. But once an individual is anatomically and physiologically mature enough for reproduction, how would that individual know whether it was sufficiently skilled to reproduce successfully? At one year of age the woodpecker can attract a mate, produce gametes, mate and lay a clutch of eggs, and successfully raise some young. It appears that all females that successfully pair with males that possess territories will attempt to breed. Some pairs do not breed, but we would need further information regarding their ages and body conditions before we could offer a full explanation for this failure. It would be difficult to establish that a pair of birds physiologically capable of breeding voluntarily declined to do so because they were inexperienced. The skill hypothesis is unattractive and difficult to endorse or reject definitively. However, if breeders disappear, for whatever reason, and they are replaced by one-year-old birds, of either sex, that breed successfully, as we know occurs with red-cockaded woodpeckers, there seems little reason to accept the skill hypothesis.

Another explanation may be termed the hard life hypothesis. It holds that environmental conditions are so poor that more than two individuals are necessary to obtain enough food, or protect against predators, to raise any young whatsoever. This explanation is not compelling. Assume that things are tough and food is scarce, so that a breeding pair can fledge only 1 offspring although they lay and hatch several eggs. Thus 2 adults produce 1 fledgling, or 0.5 fledglings each. If 1 helper allows them to fledge 2 nestlings, it is equivalent to 0.67 each, a real gain. But if the food supply is sufficient to support 2 adults plus 1 nestling but is inadequate for 2 adults plus 2 nestlings, will it truly be able to support 3 adults plus 2 nestlings? If the breeding pair could raise 2 nestlings (1 nestling each) and a helper permitted 3 to fledge, on a per capita basis production remains constant (1 nestling per adult). The male helper might as well reproduce on its own, provided a mate is available.

It is very difficult to decipher mysteries such as delayed dispersal and breeding when populations are declining. Presumably the conditions that lead to decline differ from those which fostered the evolution of cooperative breeding. For example, we can detect virtually no increase in the number of colonies today. Is this characteristic of the species or simply the result of population decline? Certainly population expansion had to occur at some point in the history of this widespread species. Young birds now pursue alternative strategies. Some disperse; others remain and help. Despite a tremendous amount of field research, we still have failed to answer the major question about this society of cooperative breeders. Is the lifetime reproductive success of males tolerating the continued presence of their male offspring greater than the lifetime reproductive success of males whose male offspring disperse?

Territories Large and Small

ANIMALS DO NOT wander aimlessly through the landscape, carrying on their lives wherever they happen to find themselves. Rather, they inhabit a prescribed space, a defined area called a home range. As they reach the perimeter of this space, they will turn back and return to familiar ground. The area can grow and shrink seasonally as the supply of temporary food resources changes. The sum of these seasonal shifts is the year-round home range. Sometimes the home ranges of individuals or groups overlap, particularly when a specific resource is abundant.

If an animal, or a group of animals, actively defends part or all of its home range, the defended area is called a territory. A territory is a more or less exclusive area which the inhabitants try to maintain all for themselves. Many animals constantly test the defenses of adjacent territories. They will deliberately wander into a neighboring territory but retreat when challenged by its rightful occupants. That part of the home range which lies beyond the defended perimeter is the extraterritorial range.

In general terms, the size of a home range or territory depends on the size of the animal living in it. Larger animals have greater metabolic requirements and thus must range over a larger area searching for food. Animals that must hunt for high-energy plant material, such as seeds, nuts, and fruits that are typically found in small clumps across the landscape, must range farther than animals that simply crop leaves and stems from the dominant vegetation. Insect-eaters and meat-eaters must range even farther to acquire sufficient food; thus top carnivores at the end of a food chain frequently have the largest home ranges of all.

Researchers have studied the home range of red-cockaded woodpeckers extensively, more than that of any other woodpecker. Because the red-cockaded woodpecker is endangered, we need to know as much as we can about its resource needs to help it survive. However, agreeing on how much foraging territory a clan of woodpeckers needs has proved to be hard for people studying the species. Determining the actual territorial boundaries of a woodpecker clan is difficult because it requires observation of contact between territorial holders and intruders to determine which group yields at a specific point in space.

On the other hand, home range is easier to determine. Published estimates of red-cockaded woodpecker home ranges have varied from 36 to 556 acres. Seven studies from four states have simply divided the acreage of a given forest by the number of clans known to inhabit the tract. Estimates have ranged from 67 to 393 acres, averaging 299 acres per clan. Since these estimates include areas which birds may not make use of, they represent maximum ranges.

Ten studies have determined the home range of one or more individual clans. The season of study and the techniques used have varied greatly, but all the studies have involved following the birds while they foraged. Joe Skorupa marked with plastic flagging each tree used for foraging by any member of a clan. After two weeks of daily tracking, he saw that the birds were using no new areas, so he mapped and measured the area of flagged trees. Others have taken aerial photographs into the field and marked their position every five minutes while following the foraging birds. Another study placed radio transmitters on one or more birds of a clan so they could be quickly located or followed from a distance. All these studies have involved color-banded birds so that individuals could be recognized and their clan membership established. The home ranges revealed by these studies varied from 35 to 526 acres, averaging 242 acres per clan.

Skorupa was the first to document seasonal expansion and contraction. Two clans doubled their foraging territory during the winter, the season of greatest food scarcity. One clan of two birds expanded from 40 acres in summer to 84 acres in winter; another went from 44 to 77 acres. In Oklahoma a clan expanded from 64 acres in spring, to 109 during summer, and to 131 acres in winter. Some clans studied did not show a seasonal shift.

A group of Forest Service researchers and cooperators has provided the most detailed study of home ranges. They studied 24 clans on prime red-cockaded woodpecker habitat at the Francis Marion National Forest and the Hobcaw Barony, both in coastal South Carolina. All but one of the clans were surrounded by neighboring clans, which theoretically would inhibit range expansion. The smallest year-round home range was 74 acres; the largest was 556 acres. Thus, even in some of the best habitat available, supporting the second-largest population anywhere—some 400 plus clans—the largest home range was more than seven times the size of the smallest. The average year-round home range was 174 acres per clan.

Some seasonal shifts were apparent. The average home range for 21 clans with nestlings was 69 acres. After the nestlings had fledged and were able to follow their parents, the home range expanded significantly to 106 acres on average. During the autumn home ranges shrank slightly to 93 acres, while in winter and early spring they averaged 121 acres. Substantial portions of the 174-acre year-round home ranges went unused for extended periods, yet the birds were able to protect the total range from usurpation by their neighbors.

Why are home ranges so variable in size? Do some contain more resources than others? Do large clans require more acres of habitat than small clans, as one would logically expect? Does an abundance of birds in a forest squeeze the size of home ranges to accommodate them all? The Forest Service researchers tested four hypotheses about home range size, with some interesting, and unexpected, results.

The first hypothesis held that home ranges would contain approximately the same quantity of foraging resources even though they differed in size. Since the woodpeckers foraged on pine trees larger than 5 inches in diameter, the researchers estimated the basal area (an estimate of space occupied by trees on an acre of forest) of pines for each home range. There was an eleven-fold difference between the minimum and the maximum pine basal area, thus foraging resource, found on the 24 home ranges. Moreover, as home range size increased, the amount of the pine resource also increased. Thus the hypothesis that all the ranges would contain the same amount of pine resource failed. Clearly some clans had access to more pines than others.

The second hypothesis tested compared home range size with the density of surrounding woodpeckers. The concept is simple and appealing. If the woodpeckers are abundant but habitat is limited, the birds will tend to be "packed in" more densely. Territorial defense will be more frequent and intense, causing territories to shrink in response. The researchers used the average distance between the nest trees of surrounding clans to estimate bird density. Other workers who studied the home ranges of 4 clans elsewhere in South Carolina had reported that the size of the home range shrank as population density increased. This study demonstrated the same phenomenon. The researchers found between 1 and 22 active clans within 1¼ miles of the nest tree of each clan studied and discovered a strong inverse relationship between home range size and population density.

The third hypothesis suggested that the quality of habitat determined home range size. Young pine trees and hardwood trees of all ages occupy space which is of little, if any, benefit to red-cockaded woodpeckers. Home ranges may have to increase if substantial amounts of young pines or hardwoods constitute the habitat. On the other hand, old large pine trees represent a high-quality habitat that may permit a reduction in home range size. When tested, this hypothesis could not be rejected, but habitat quality did not appear to be an important determinant of home range size for the 24 clans studied.

The final hypothesis tested the relationship between the number of birds in a clan and its home range size. This seemed to be the most reasonable causal relationship of all. If 1 bird requires so many acres of foraging habitat, then 2 birds should require twice that amount and so on. But how big is a clan? If we start with a pair of adults, and they fledge 4 youngsters, we have tripled clan size. For the first month the adults capture and bring all food for the nestlings. Ideally, adequate food resources would exist close to the nest tree so the adults can efficiently ferry food to the nestlings, though the birds may rapidly deplete local resources this way. However, as the youngsters fledge, they can follow the adults farther afield to more abundant resources. As the fledglings learn to capture their own food, they need food abundantly available because they are such inefficient hunters.

Over the winter all the female offspring, and perhaps half the male offspring, will disperse to other areas beyond the home range perimeter. Other males may remain as helpers. Clan size can therefore vary substantially over the year, and the home range needs to be large enough to accommodate all the potential residents. Before nesting, the 24 clans in the study averaged 2.6 birds per clan, ranging from 2 to 5 birds each. After nesting, there were 4.3 birds per clan, ranging from 2 to 9 birds each. There was no significant relationship between the average monthly size of the group and the size of the year-round home range occupied by the group. While 12 clans without helpers averaged 168 acres, 12 clans with helpers averaged 179 acres, an insignificant difference. However, if population density of surrounding clans also was considered, the size of the group was significantly related to home range size. There was little evidence that group size influenced the home range occupied at any particular season of the year.

This study demonstrated that red-cockaded woodpeckers exhibit territoriality toward their neighbors throughout the year and that territorial boundaries were quite distinct. Home range size varied widely; apparently groups in a local area simply divided the available habitat among themselves. This arrangement implies that it could be quite difficult for young woodpeckers to establish their own territories in an environment with limited habitat resources.

We have learned much from these studies, but we still face a number of intriguing questions. If 30 or 35 acres of habitat are adequate to support some birds, why are other home ranges as large as 500 to 550 acres? Even in the same prime coastal forest the largest home range for a given season was 5 times greater than the smallest.

How do red-cockaded woodpecker home ranges compare with those of other woodpeckers? Unfortunately woodpecker biologists have not been interested in this aspect for other species. A. W. Reller studied red-headed and red-bellied woodpeckers in hardwood forests of Illinois; she found 8 pairs of red-headed and 5 pairs of red-bellied woodpeckers in a 31-acre oak-hickory forest. In a 37-acre oak-maple forest, she found 13 pairs of red-headed and 2 pairs of red-bellied wood-peckers. These mast-feeding, omnivorous woodpeckers can obviously get by with less than 10 acres of habitat.

A 12-year study of a 30-acre hardwood forest in Maryland found 1 to 3 pairs of red-bellied, 2 to 3 pairs of downy, and occasionally 1 pair of hairy woodpeckers in residence. Similar studies indicate that red-bellied woodpeckers typically use 12 acres, downy woodpeckers use 15 acres, hairy woodpeckers use 20 acres, and flickers use 21 acres. Another study of hairy woodpeckers found winter territories as small as 15 acres.

Tanner studied the ivory-billed woodpecker in the bottom-land forests of Louisiana and determined the maximum density for 3 woodpeckers there. He found 21 pairs of red-bellied woodpeckers per square mile (30 acres per pair), 6 pairs of pileated woodpeckers per square mile (107 acres per pair), and 1 pair of ivory-billed woodpeckers per 6 square miles (3,840 acres per pair). The black woodpecker of Eurasia, a slightly larger close relative of the pileated woodpecker, seems to have territories as variable as the red-cockaded. It has territories of 300 to 445 acres in Bohemia, 740 to 1,235 acres in France, 620 to 1,480 acres in Germany, 2,100 acres in the Netherlands, and 2,000 to 4,400 acres in Finland.

The red-cockaded woodpecker clearly requires an exceptionally large home range for a bird of its size. Even if the prime habitat average of 174 acres per clan is considered "typical" for the species over its entire geographic distribution, we must remember that an average range would accommodate only one-half of the clans. If a forest manager hopes to provide sufficient foraging habitat to meet the home range requirement for 85 percent of the clans, 262 acres will be needed. This large but indispensable home range requirement complicates strategies to save the species.

Bits and Pieces

THREE INTERRELATED CHANGES in the forests it inhabits have contributed to the current plight of the red-cockaded woodpecker. First, the total area of forested land across its range has shrunk. Second, the forests of many species that have regenerated in the wake of the turn-of-the-century timber harvests are rapidly giving way to even-aged stands of monoculture pine plantations. Finally, agricultural, industrial, recreational, and urban development continues to fragment the remaining forests into ever-diminishing, isolated patches.

Some 188 million acres of commercial forest, occupying 37 percent of the landscape, stretch across the South (here the coastal tier of states from Texas to Virginia plus Oklahoma,

161

Arkansas, and Tennessee). Pine forests cover 63 million acres (34 percent), but only 1.6 million acres (2.5 percent) are old enough (60 plus years) to serve as red-cockaded woodpecker nesting habitat. Of this potential habitat of trees 60 years of age or older, only one-fourth is prime habitat of 80 years or older. The preferred pine species, longleaf and slash pines, are declining 3 times more rapidly than loblolly and shortleaf pine habitat because forest owners prefer to replace longleaf with faster-growing species.

Although 75 percent of suitable red-cockaded woodpecker habitat is privately owned, as many as 84 percent of all wood-pecker colonies exist on federal lands. The bulk of colonies on federal lands, 80 percent, are located in the national for-ests, which typically are disjunct, with many private inhold-ings. Thus the existing woodpecker habitat stands in isolated patches. Disjunct habitat fragments and development of in-tervening lands disrupt processes of dispersal and genetic in-terchange. Rates of extinction tend to run high among species that reside in small, fragmented habitats.

If the bulk of forestlands is in private hands, why have the woodpeckers been disappearing from these forests? A recent study of Texas forests provides some insight. Of 26 million acres of wooded land in Texas, 11.6 million acres can be considered commercial timberland, all located in the 43 east-ern counties referred to as the pineywoods. While total tim-berland acreage has remained stable (less than 1 percent loss) in recent years, pine and pine-hardwood forests have declined 8 percent since 1975. The greatest loss has occurred in the nonindustrial, privately owned forests, which constitute 61 percent of the forested land. On these lands, pine forests have shrunk by 16 percent.

Two factors have led to this decline. Many nonindustrial private landowners (farmers, individuals, and corporations) harvest their trees without making effort to replace the trees they remove. They simply accept whatever tree species regen-erate naturally, replanting only 6 out of every 100 harvested acres. They do cut fewer trees than industrial forest owners, although one-third of the nonindustrial acreage was harvested between 1975 and 1986. Nonindustrial owners are also far less likely to clear-cut their timber; only 1 out of 5 acres was harvested in this fashion. But they are more likely to remove only the best pine trees, leaving poorly formed pines and less valuable hardwoods to dominate the forest. When pine forests (that is, forests composed of 50 percent or more pine trees) were cut, only 3 out of 5 acres successfully established a new pine generation. When pine-hardwood forests (25 to 49 percent pine trees) were harvested, only 1 out of 5 acres established a new pine generation.

Management practices for the industrial private forests can be even more devastating to red-cockaded woodpeckers. More than half these lands in Texas were harvested between 1975 and 1986, resulting in massive conversion to pine plantations, with 1.5 million acres planted. Think of planting a piece of Texas larger than the state of Delaware to pine trees in just eleven years. More than half the harvested forest was clearcut; think of it as razing the state of Rhode Island. Most of the industrial land is managed with short harvest rotations which maximize the production of fiber, such as pulpwood or chips. The production of slow-growing, close-grained, high-quality sawtimber is not as profitable. This places more pressure on the public national forests to provide sawtimber, particularly to harvest the existing 50- to 70-year-old middle-aged trees. Because of public "demand" for sawtimber, national forest managers resist extending harvest rotations to 80 to 100 years, which would most benefit the woodpeckers.

Even the nonindustrial private forests which are not harvested have become less hospitable habitats for red-cockaded woodpeckers. These landowners seldom burn their forests. As a result, hardwood seedlings and saplings, which would perish in even moderately hot fires, persist and mature. They first dominate the forest floor, forming dense thickets below the woodpeckers, which seldom descend to the ground. In time these hardwoods also dominate the mid-story, the tree layer beneath the crowns of the tallest trees. Here they become a major impediment to the woodpeckers, blocking the entrances to cavities and diminishing the open flight space between trees. This growth changes the overall appearance of the forest. Red-cockaded woodpeckers prefer open, parklike forests, where they can see some distance in all directions and easily fly about, below the tree crowns and between the trunks. As hardwoods come to dominate the forest, this openness disappears, and the birds can neither see nor travel through the dense hardwood treetops. Large suitable pine trees may still exist, but the forest no longer provides a good habitat for the woodpeckers.

How have these forestry trends affected the woodpeckers in Texas? Originally found in 40 counties, the birds currently persist in only 9. Texas law prohibits disturbance and destruction of red-cockaded woodpecker nest sites, but no protection exists for forest habitat in the vicinity of the nest trees. In other words, a private landowner can cut down every tree except the nest tree and violate no state statute.

Texas Parks and Wildlife Department employees accumulated information regarding woodpecker colonies on private land between 1968 and 1977. They identified 31 colonies on 21 different tracts of land. When these colonies were revisited between 1985 and 1987, no colonies were found on 17 of the tracts, where 19 colonies formerly existed. Of the 12 original colonies on the remaining 4 tracts of forest, 9 survived. Over the course of 10 years 71 percent of the colonies had disappeared. Clearcutting of forest habitat and nesting trees was responsible for the loss of 19 colonies. Mid-story encroachment and death of relic trees accounted for the three additional colonies lost.

The fragmentation of the red-cockaded woodpecker's habitat is occurring at several different levels. At the regional level land use changes are causing the birds to disappear from private lands and leaving widely separated national forest islands as the only areas of livable habitat. Within the national forest landscape, the woodpecker subpopulations are further fragmented by small holdings of private land, water bodies, riverine hardwood forests, or large regenerated areas too young to support the birds. Finally, within the thousand-acre national forest compartments, clearcutting practices restrict the birds to tiny islands, narrow peninsulas, or other limited areas. Birds that typically confine their dispersal to adjacent clan territories may suddenly find themselves without neighbors as harvest practices eliminate adjacent territories altogether.

People frequently assert that clearcutting mimics natural forest processes, such as catastrophic fires and storm blowdowns that eliminate forest canopies and restart forest succession in patches of various size. This analogy is incorrect. In old-growth forests such catastrophes were infrequent and seldom affected more than 10 percent of a large forest tract at any given point in time. The result was isolated clearings widely dispersed in a forest matrix. Today the reverse is true. The isolates are the islands of old-growth forest, not the forest clearings. Clearcutting forces the woodpeckers to seek out the scattered old-growth islands in a sea of inhospitable young forest or pine plantations. This is very different from avoiding island clearings in a broad old-growth forest, and the consequences are rather drastic.

This change in the ratio of old-growth and mature pine forest to young second growth is a crucial issue. Physical changes follow forest fragmentation; paramount among these is the edge effect. Trees in a thick forest stand grow in a particular way precisely because of this stand. Root systems have been inhibited from expansion by the close proximity of adjacent tree roots, all competing for the same space, water, and nutrients. But harbored in the midst of the forest, these trees enjoy shelter from strong winds and narrow root systems are adequate. Clearcutting instantly changes the tree's environment by creating a distinct edge. On one side lies the forest; on the other, bare ground or a grassland. This represents the starkest distinction in habitat that forest animals and plants can encounter.

Suddenly trees at the forest edge are exposed to wind and sunlight they have never experienced. A useful rule of thumb holds that the climatic effects of a clearcut extend into the forest approximately three tree heights. For southern pines, this may be 250 to 300 feet. This rule of thumb has far-reaching effects. Let us assume that a 300-foot buffer zone adjacent to the edge is required to negate the edge effects. Consider a circle, which has the least amount of edge per unit of area. A 300-foot-radius circle will be 100 percent buffer zone encompassing 6.5 acres. Doubling the size of the circle, the 300-foot-wide edge zone now occupies 19 acres, leaving 6.5 acres in the middle free of edge effect. It requires a circle of 1,050-foot radius, with 80 acres of area, to protect an area of central forest equal to the exposed buffer zone.

Exposure of the forest edge to wind and sunlight also increases evaporation, leading to a drier surface litter. This, in turn, lessens the pace of pine needle and deciduous leaf decomposition, slowing nutrient recycling. The dry surface soil and litter, perhaps augmented by a spell of reduced precipitation, may exacerbate damaging southern pine beetle outbreaks. The drier conditions certainly increase the risk of damaging wildfire. These are some of the potential ramifications of forest management practices spiraling ever outward from clearcutting alone. Everything is connected to everything else.

Forest birds generally fall into two categories, interior species and edge species. Interior species can find their life requisites only within the forest interior, their primary habitat. Edge species tend to be commonplace generalists that can locate their survival needs in diverse habitats. In general, hole-nesting and bark-foraging birds tend to be more abundant in old-growth, interior forest stands. Red-cockaded woodpeckers do best in open but old-growth forests. Forest edges function as secondary habitats for them, providing some, but not all, of their life requisites. Hole-nesting edge species, such as red-headed woodpeckers, flickers, bluebirds, and starlings, thrive along forest edges and greatly increase competition for red-cockaded woodpecker cavities. Thus habitat fragmentation, particularly as a result of clearcut harvesting, puts a double whammy on the red-cockaded woodpeckers. First, it physically reduces usable habitat available to the birds, perhaps limiting their territory and certainly reducing their food resources. And second, it attracts edge species to the newly created edges and increases competition for the remaining nest cavities.

Thus the red-cockaded woodpecker is a species being nibbled to death. Its habitat is forever being divided into bits and pieces until finally there won't be enough left. Harvest and windfall will claim more and more cavity trees, or competitors will evict the birds. Hardwoods will continue to invade pine stands as fire is suppressed and sunlight within the forest increases. The species will have survived the turn-of-the-century pillaging of the pine forests only to succumb to "modern" forest management.

CHAPTER NINE

Beetlemania

IN ONE RESPECT a tree, being anchored to the ground, represents little more than a target. It must endure insults and injuries from all sorts of unwelcome guests and squatters. In recent years scientists have come to understand that most of the exotic chemicals which trees produce, harbor, and release in response to certain stimuli are actually potent weapons in an elaborate defense system. A single species of pine tree may be attacked by more than two hundred species of insects. Because a defense developed against one of these insects may be ineffective against another, it is not surprising that no tree has successfully erected a total defense against all its enemies.

Trees have thus had to participate in active chemical warfare for millions of years as they and their insect enemies have evolved defenses and counterdefenses while locked in slow mortal combat.

Pines have existed in North America for 100 million years. Pine forests cover 132 million acres of the United States today, nearly one-fifth of all forested land. There are six major pine forest types. The ponderosa pine, lodgepole pine, and western white pine ecosystems exist from the Rocky Mountains westward. The white-red-jack pine ecosystem is found in the north-central and northeastern United States. The loblolly-shortleaf pine ecosystem, the largest of the six, occurs over much of the eastern half of the nation. The longleaf-slash pine ecosystem is restricted to the southeastern and south-central Atlantic coastal plain.

Beetles are the most common form of life known, with 290,000 species scattered around the earth, 10 percent occurring in North America. A number of species specialize in feeding on pine trees: ambrosia beetles, turpentine beetles, pine sawyers, engraver beetles, and pine beetles. Pine forests have persisted because they have evolved effective defense mechanisms to counter beetle attacks. But pine trees, like humans, become more susceptible to attack by parasites and pathogens when they are under stress. Stress for trees can take the form of drought, fire, lack of nutrients, too many trees growing too close together, injury, or attack by too many insects at one time.

While other kinds of insects focus on eating the emerging needles of pine trees, beetles concentrate on penetrating the bark and tunneling through the soft cambium tissues which produce new tree growth and are rich in nutrients. Some beetle larvae feed communally, eating away a large shallow chamber which eventually fills with frass, their fecal material. Other species construct individual chambers which form a characteristic pattern beneath the bark: Some tunnel downward; some create Y- or H-shaped galleries; others create S-shaped chambers that intersect one another and gradually girdle the tree, killing it.

Pine bark beetles of the genus *Dendroctonus* are major pests of pine forests wherever they are found. The western pine beetle is the most destructive insect in the ponderosa pine ecosystem. The mountain pine beetle substantially damages lodgepole pine forests. The southern pine beetle wreaks the most havoc in the loblolly-shortleaf pine ecosystem. None of these beetles operates alone. For example, the southern pine beetle must compete with the black turpentine beetle (another *Dendroctonus* species) and three species of *Ips* engraver beetles in its own backyard. Together these five species pose a formidable obstacle to the production of loblolly pines. For several decades most attention has focused on the southern pine beetle, which has caused multimillion-dollar losses to the timber and fiber industry.

Southern pine beetles, at first glance, would seem innocuous. A mere eighth of an inch long, this type of beetle is rarely ever seen. Its reproductive cycle begins when an adult female beetle begins searching for a suitable pine tree to attack. A pine tree weakened by lightning, drought, wind and ice damage, human-caused injuries, or stress from any factor is an acceptable target. When the female finds a suitable host, she begins to chew a hole through the bark. While boring into the tree, the female releases a pheromone, called frontalin, and another chemical, trans-verbenol, which enhances the effect of frontalin. Pheromones are chemicals which, even in minute quantities, stimulate response from other individuals of the same species. In this instance the message is directed toward male beetles; the message is "Ya'll come!" The males, detecting single molecules of frontalin wafting by on gentle air currents, immediately head upwind, seeking stronger and stronger stimuli. They zero in on the tunnel, which is a mere one twenty-fifth of an inch in diameter. Inside, the female continues to burrow, emitting audible chirps to guide the male into her hidden bridal bower.

As the male enters the female's chamber, the chemical games continue. He starts emitting verbenone, a different pheromone, which inhibits the attractiveness of frontalin to other males. This message gives notice to the next arriving male that he is too late, that another suitor has already responded to the lady's beckoning. The male also releases endobrevicomin, which will inhibit newly arriving females. The pine tree responds to these attacks by releasing volatile alphapinene compounds, which unfortunately seem to attract even more beetles. But as more females bore in, and more males respond, increasing concentrations of verbenone and endobrevicomin cause newly arriving females to veer away in search of other host trees, and males to veer off in search of unmated females. Thousands of beetles may attack a single tree, averaging 35 pairs of beetles to a single square foot of tree bark. The initial attack usually occurs in the middle of the trunk. As the aggregation of beetles increases, new arrivals disperse to the upper and lower trunk and branches.

As the females bore through the bark and reach the sapwood of the tree, they mate and begin construction of galleries in which they can lay eggs. As she progresses, the female chews small niches in the side of the gallery and lays a single tiny egg in each. After laying as many as 30 eggs, the female tunnels her way back to the surface of the tree and emerges to seek a new host tree and repeat the process. Each females is able to produce 2 or 3 broods of eggs. The eggs hatch in 3 to 11 days, depending on temperature, and the larvae begin to tunnel away from the gallery, filling their excavation with frass behind them. The larvae chew and burrow their merry way for 15 to 40 days, growing faster at higher environmental temperatures, and then tunnel away from the trunk into the bark. Having grown to a quarter inch in length as larvae, they are now ready to pupate and transform their soft white bodies

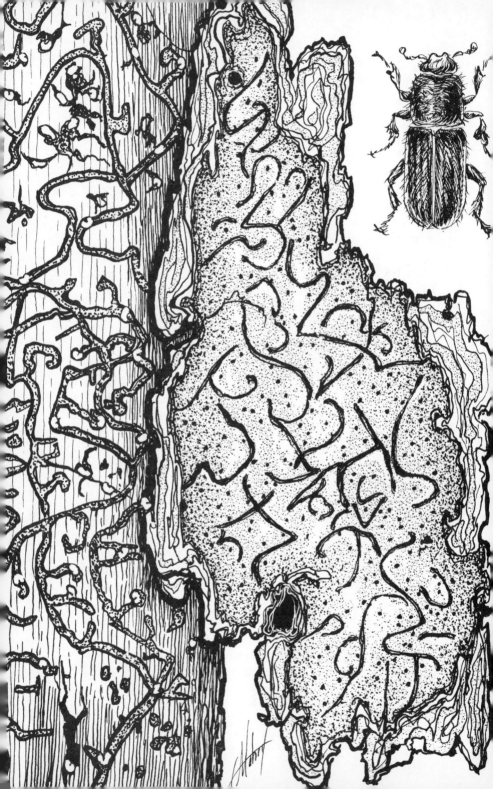

into the smaller, hard, brown, winged adult stage. Once this stage is completed, the new adults tunnel to the surface, emerge, and seek a new host tree to repeat the cycle.

A new generation of southern pine beetles can arise in 30 to 75 days. Beetles along the colder, northern edge of its distribution can produce 2 or 3 generations in a single year. Along the Gulf coast, the milder climate fosters a longer reproductive season, and 7 to 9 generations may result. Because it is not uncommon for a cohort of beetles to increase their numbers tenfold in a single generation, a pair of beetles could theoretically mate and initiate the production of 20 million or more beetles in seven generations before winter terminates the breeding season.

In this century the southern pine beetle populations have erupted about every ten years or so. The epidemics have persisted for one to three years before subsiding from natural causes, which are poorly understood. Between the epidemics the beetles may be so scarce as to be hard to find. During eruptions, with their tremendous reproductive potential, as noted above, the beetles may become so abundant that they kill thousands of pine trees. We have yet to answer satisfactorily two critical questions: Why do low, endemic populations erupt periodically into epidemics and why do epidemics subside?

Most parasites and pathogens are prudent. It behooves them to be so. After all, if you are dependent upon a host organism for your livelihood, it is not in your best interest to kill your host. The presence of a parasite can weaken or irritate a host, but as long as the host continues to function, it will provide nutrients and shelter to its unwanted guests. In general, parasites and their hosts coevolve a semibalanced relationship. The host develops defenses which prevent the parasite from totally overwhelming it, and the parasite suc-

FIGURE 9-1 Larval and adult southern pine beetles and their feeding galleries. The actual length of the adult beetle is $\frac{1}{8}$ inch.

cessfully evades the defenses frequently enough to persist as a viable population. Were this not so, either host or parasite would be in grave danger of extinction. Epidemics happen when a parasite or pathogen besieges a new host, one unaccustomed and defenseless to its attack, or when the parasites gain a significant environmental advantage. Fossil evidence indicates that pines have been present in North America for 100 million years, and the bark beetles for 50 million years. It would appear they have had ample time to accommodate themselves to each other, and both are still abundant.

Bark beetles are unique parasites because they kill the pine tree they infest. The pine tree depends on the quantity and quality of oleoresin in the tree sap to defend itself. When beetle excavation punctures the resin canals, the resin is forced into the beetle's burrow, sometimes trapping and immobilizing the insect, and seeping onto the surface of the tree trunk to form a "pitch tube," a telltale sign of beetle presence. Healthy pines have ample pitch under high pressure which will quickly fill entrance tunnels and galleries, preventing the beetles from mating and laying eggs. Weak and injured trees cannot repel the beetle attack, particularly when large numbers of beetles simultaneously attack a tree, as happens during epidemic outbreaks.

The pine bark beetles have enlisted the assistance of certain microorganisms, particularly the blue stain fungus, to aid in killing the tree. The fungi and other microbes live on the outer surface of both male and female beetles. Fungi usually cannot penetrate a tree surface; they require a broken limb or mechanical injury on the tree to gain access to interior tissues. The beetle provides entry into the most desirable tissue, the living cells between bark and sapwood. Once inside, the fungus quickly spreads and helps kill the tree, aiding the beetle—a mutually beneficial symbiosis.

The southern pine beetle can successfully attack and kill a number of different pine species. Its preferred hosts, as judged by those species in which epidemics most frequently develop, are the loblolly and shortleaf pines. But the geographic range of the beetle exceeds the range of those two pine species, and the beetle also attacks pitch pine, Virginia pine, pond pine, slash pine, longleaf pine, Table-mountain pine, spruce pine, red pine, Apache pine, eastern white pine, and several spruces, plus four additional pines in Central America. In other words, it has very catholic tastes. Attacks against white pine and spruce trees are rare and successful only when large numbers of beetles are available from a nearby primary host. It is significant that longleaf and slash pines, the copious resin producers favored by the naval stores industry and red-cockaded woodpeckers, have strong defenses against beetle attacks and typically succumb only when large numbers of beetles have reached outbreak densities on other pine species nearby.

The picture that emerges from this discussion indicates that healthy trees can hold their own against a few beetles. As more beetles are attracted to, and attack, a single tree, sheer numbers can overwhelm even a healthy tree. The success of any attack will be greater if the tree has suffered any injury, weakening, or stress. A sufficient number of weakened trees will always be present in a forest to perpetuate the survival of a beetle population. The question therefore becomes: What conditions lead to an epidemic outbreak of beetles? With their tremendous reproductive potential, increasing an order of magnitude with each generation, and capable of 2 to 9 generations per year, what other forces keep these populations in check?

All organisms, including humans, can reproduce fast enough to outstrip their environmental resources. The external forces discussed in Chapter Three—competition, predation, resource loss, and environmental change—prevent them from doing so. These four external, thus environmental, forces check the explosive reproductive potential of most organisms. This counterplay is what we generally term the balance of nature.

Which of these forces, or combination of them, is playing a dominant role in populations dynamics of the southern pine beetle? Competitors, in the form of the four other beetles already mentioned, undoubtedly exist. However, the southern pine beetle dominates this beetle guild and apparently causes far greater damage to pine forests than do the other species. These beetles compete for the same resource, pine trees, but are unlikely to interfere with one another in doing so, in the sense that the actions of one species directly interfere with the biological success of another species. All are endemic to the southern pine forests, and we have no indication that the actions of one species prevent or cause a surging epidemic of another species. Competition within the beetle guild in these forests is unlikely to be a "release factor" that leads to southern pine beetle outbreaks.

Southern pine beetles live out their entire life cycle in southern pine trees, making the supply of pines susceptible to invasion a critical resource. The beetle and the pines have coexisted for thousands of years without either's becoming extinct. Even during epidemics the beetles do not infect all pine trees. Although a sizable patch of forest may succumb, a few trees within the patch, and many trees around the patch, resist the beetle attack. These trees reseed the patch, and the pine forest persists. But a forest need not disappear to affect the pine beetle cycle. Changes in the forest population characteristics, such as the age structure, or demography, of the forest, will suffice. Vigorous young trees better repel pine beetle attacks, as do healthy mature trees. Old trees, like humans, lose their vigor and become more susceptible to infection. As a forest ages, the risk of a pine beetle epidemic increases.

Strangely enough, the density of a stand of pine trees can contribute to the start of a beetle outbreak. A mature pine produces a carpet of seedlings beneath its boughs. Those seedlings that receive adequate light and nutrients will persist and grow, though most will succumb, unable to compete with the parent tree and surrounding plants. Should the large trees be harvested or killed by beetles and other natural causes, the seedlings or saplings will be "released" for a spurt of growth, basking in the sunlight and nutrient pool. As this cohort of new trees matures, competition for light and nutrients will intensify, and a dense stand of spindly trees may result. As their health declines, they become increasingly likely candidates for beetle infection. Thus, while competition between coexistent beetles may not affect the southern pine beetle success, competition among their hosts can weaken certain individual trees and stimulate a beetle outbreak.

A direct change in the physical environmental can also spur a beetle outbreak. A prolonged drought, an unusual freeze, or an ice storm may weaken trees over a large area, but beetle outbreaks in recent decades have covered a much larger expanse of the nation. No one has found a connection between long-term climatic change and the beetle eruptions. We can safely eliminate this type of environmental change as the culprit.

The final environmental factor to be considered is predation. Belief in the substantial effect of consumers on populations of plants or animals lower in a food chain has an illustrious history in ecological theory. The results, though, are rather mixed, as we might expect. Some predators, including grazers that consume plants unable to run away, appear to have absolutely no effect upon their prey populations. Other consumers seem to have drastic impact and may even regulate the absolute numbers of their prey. Certainly southern pine beetles do not lack for natural enemies. Clerid beetles home in on the pheromones released by the pine beetles and attack the adults. The clerids also lay their eggs in the same trees, and the clerid larvae feed on the pine beetle larvae. Tenebrionid beetles are often abundant in pine beetle-infested trees. These beetles are principally scavengers, feeding on pine beetle frass and the blue stain fungi, but when they chance upon pine beetle eggs and larvae in the galleries, they consume these also. Predaceous bugs, flies, and cylindrical bark beetles also prey on pine beetles.

Mites commonly infest pine beetles. Some mites may directly reduce the physical health of the beetles while others may be a mere nuisance. The general abundance of mites associated with the beetles indicates that they may influence beetle populations to some degree, but little data suggest they have a large effect on beetle populations. A variety of pathogens, including bacteria, fungi, nematodes, protozoans, and microsporidians, are known to infect pine beetles. But we do not yet know how important these pathogens and predators are in controlling the beetle populations or contributing to their outbreaks.

Leaping to organisms several orders of magnitude larger than pine beetles, we find that birds, particularly several species of woodpeckers, are important natural enemies of pine beetles. The birds feed directly on the insects, and it takes many tiny beetles to make a decent meal for these warm-blooded predators. Woodpeckers shift their foraging activity into stands of pines attacked during beetle outbreaks. Scaling off the outer layers of bark, they expose beetle larvae and pupae in their galleries. Even beetles that the birds do not expose and consume are affected because removal of bark contributes to the desiccation of beetles hidden from view. Woodpeckers feed most heavily on beetles in the summer and fall, when beetle populations are highest, but the impact of woodpecker predation may be greater during the winter. Woodpeckers consume a smaller percentage of available beetles during the summer, when beetles are superabundant, than they do in winter, when the beetles lie dormant and alternative prey is less available. Woodpeckers steadily munching on beetles all winter result in a much smaller population of beetles ready to reproduce come spring. This interaction between birds and beetles will be explored further in the following chapter.

178

Thus far we have examined several factors which may affect the rise and fall of beetle populations, but all from the same perspective: the effect of each factor on the beetles. But the beetles are an integral part of the pine forest ecosystem. Perhaps we can gain some insight into the question of beetle outbreaks if we also examine the role of the beetles within their ecosystems. After all, we have three closely related species of the same genus each filling a very similar niche in three different pine ecosystems: the western pine beetle in the ponderosa pine ecosystem, the mountain pine beetle in the lodgepole pine ecosystem, and the southern pine beetle in the loblolly-shortleaf pine ecosystem. We know that the beetles and pines have coexisted for millions of years, at least 40 million. Even one outbreak every 100 years means that 400,000 outbreaks may have occurred without exterminating the pines. How do these outbreaks affect the forest ecosystem as a whole?

A successful beetle attack will kill the pine tree. The trees most often attacked are the older and larger trees. Following an outbreak, the size structure and composition of the forest can be changed significantly, depending on the successional stage of the forest. Recall that pines are a pioneer species that do best in the full, open sunshine. As they grow and shade the forest floor, the shade-loving hardwood trees can sprout and persist. While hardwoods grow and dominate the forest canopy overhead, young pine seedlings fail to thrive in the dense shade. As several hundred years go by, the forest undergoes a transition from pine to pine-hardwood to total hardwood forest.

The death of a small clump of pines from pine beetles can lead to several outcomes, depending on the location and soil of the site. If the pine trees were a minor component of the forest in that area, because of a low-lying wet location or advanced succession, hardwoods would likely replace the trees killed by beetles, benefiting from a limited increase in light and reduced root competition, and succession would accelerate. If pines were a major component of the forest at that site, the additional light and reduced root competition would allow pine seedlings to enjoy a period of rapid growth. If poor soil and a dry, sandy ridge site meant that pines were the only species capable of growing there, the pine forest would certainly persist.

Beetle-killed pine trees remain standing for many years. They attract a horde of microbes and animal species that feed voraciously, even audibly, on decomposing wood and bark and on each other. Initially the trees attract pine beetle parasites and predators that feed on the abundant burrowing larvae. As the trees decompose and soften, those woodpeckers unable, or unwilling, to carve out cavities in living pines find suitable cavity sites everywhere, and the dead trees quickly become pocked with nest and roost holes of all sizes to accommodate the local woodpecker guild. Although all the dead trees eventually will fall to the ground, it is a protracted affair, a twig here, a branch there, a wind-tossed trunk in exposed locales. The recycling of nutrients in a forest is a slow and gradual process. Except for the initial drop of pine needles as the trees die, no rapid buildup of flammable material on the forest floor occurs.

The southeastern pine forests experience one of the highest incidences of electrical storms in the world, averaging 50 to 80 storm days each year. Lightning-scarred tree trunks are common throughout the region. Once ignited, a fire in the primeval forest might have persisted for days, burning a large expanse of woodlands before expiring. Seedlings, both pine and hardwood, would likely have perished. Pine saplings, growing rapidly, may have gotten their needles above the forest floor out of harm's way. Hardwood saplings, growing slowly, would perish if the interval between fires were too short. The result would be a thinning of the young pine trees and near elimination of the hardwoods, favoring persistence of the pinewoods as forest succession was set back time and again.

The North American Indians may have increased the frequency of fires, for they deliberately set forest fires to control brush and favor the herbaceous vegetation preferred by deer. Otherwise they did little to affect the size or frequency of lightning-ignited fires. The coming of Europeans did change the nature of lightning-ignited fires. As horses and wagons began to carve out roads through the forest, trampling the ancient foot trails, each roadway, rutted and denuded of vegetation, created a fire barrier. Linked to agricultural fields as civilization advanced, the acreage burned by each forest fire gradually shrank. This trend culminated in the asphalt spider web of roads which today facilitates the rapid transport of fire fighters homing on every plume of smoke on the horizon. Assiduously stomping out each blaze, these smoke eaters are unaware of the changing forest about them. In the absence of fire, pine seedlings form a carpet of "grass" beneath their progenitors, creating dense, spindly thickets of saplings. Hardwoods persist until their leaf-bearing crowns are safe above the forest floor. Once their vulnerable leaves are above the fire zone, the hardwoods spread their limbs to create a new layer of vegetation, forming a mid-story where none existed and taking a giant step toward the hardwood climax forest.

The pine bark beetles, dependent upon the pine forest, helped maintain the forest of fire-climax pinewoods. An outbreak of beetles would lead to a substantial kill of pine trees, opening up the forest canopy to more sunlight and heat than the hardwoods could withstand. Pine seedlings and saplings, suddenly released from competition and provided ample sunshine, would soon dominate the regenerating forest.

Researchers at the University of Washington have deciphered a complex puzzle of nearly identical nature on the West Coast. Lodgepole pines can grow on infertile volcanic pumice soils found in Oregon. Once established, the pines periodically experience forest fires. If fire damage is severe enough, scars which are detectable many years later when the trees are cut, form on the trunk. Trees which have fire scars are also more likely to be infected with a fungus, *Phaeolus schweinitzii*, which enters the tree through fire-caused wounds. The fungus spreads very slowly, but after 30 to 100 years of infection, it can produce large areas of advanced decay.

Advanced fungal decay weakens the trees and lowers their resistance to the mountain pine beetle, *Dendroctonus ponderosae*, which attacks both healthy and fungal-infected trees. The fungus appears to oxidize the beetle pheromone alpha-pinene to form trans-verbenol. The increased amount of trans-verbenol signals other dispersing pine beetles that a susceptible tree is available. A massive beetle attack then succeeds in killing the fire-scarred host tree. For a few years following the pine beetle outbreak, the beetle-killed trees fall to the forest floor and provide a large amount of potential fuel. Lightning will eventually ignite the forest, and a hot fire will result. The fire will release the nutrients contained in the dead trees, thus stimulating new growth in this nutrient-deficient soil as the surviving pine trees reseed the area. A whole new age-class of ponderosa pines starts growing on the burned spot, creating a patch of even-aged trees. The surviving trees which were scarred by the fire are infected by the fungus, and a whole new cycle is set in motion, to culminate in another mountain pine beetle outbreak in 80 to 100 years.

Before we move on, let us reflect a moment. The foregoing reflects conventional wisdom regarding pine beetle biology. But something seems amiss. Most parasites are prudent. The conventional view that the number of pine beetles attacking a pine tree must be sufficient to kill the tree would seem to indicate that these parasites are definitely imprudent. Are we perhaps asking the wrong questions or misinterpreting the answers? Pine beetles are always present in pine forests. In most years they are present at endemic population levels, fewer than 1 beetle per square meter of pine tree surface. During these normal years they may be difficult even to find.

Epidemic populations, more than 80 beetles per square meter, occur in rare outbursts, years apart. Thus outbreaks may be considered abnormal. From a narrow viewpoint, the sole function of a beetle is to pass on its genes to the next generation. The generation times are the same in both endemic and epidemic years, measured in days. So during the endemic years the beetles are quietly going about their business of attracting or locating the opposite sex and guaranteeing the next generation. They do this quite successfully and without killing the pine tree they select for that purpose. Were this not true, they would quickly go extinct. The beetles are, in fact, prudent.

Southern pine beetles have an effective communication system. The female pheromones signal males at great distances, while her audible chirps lead the first to arrive into her boudoir. They are positive signals. The male pheromone warns the next to arrive that he is too late, advising him to direct his attentions elsewhere, to find another female advertising her wares. This is a negative feedback signal. Generation follows generation, year after year, without pine tree fatalities. Sporadically, at lengthy intervals, something goes wrong. Perhaps a number of environmental variables all turn positive simultaneously. Too many beetle eggs develop into adults. Too many adults attack the same tree, causing its death. Too many trees die, creating an open patch in the forest canopy and fuel on the forest floor. The patch admits sunlight, and a new generation of pines erupt from the earth. A fire may eventually reduce or eliminate hardwoods competing for the same sunshine. In this way the life of the pine ecosystem is extended.

Is this scenario realistic? Are the beetles a necessary component of the pine ecosystem life cycle? Do beetles really have to kill the pine which they target? Right now it remains a mystery, but someday we may understand why pine beetle epidemics subside. Perhaps at that moment we will have learned to phrase the right question.

Pine beetle epidemics are a fact of forest life, perhaps even necessary. The U.S. Forest Service typically reacts to them in panic-stricken horror. All those dead trees, wasted! Well, not really. A tree killed by the beetles is no deader than a tree cut by a logger. The beetles have barely penetrated the surface of the tree, that portion discarded by the sawmill anyway. No loss is suffered for trees destined to become wood chips or fiber. If the beetle-killed trees are expediently harvested, before they have decayed, the loggers lose nothing. Pine beetle epidemics certainly disrupt harvest planning, but this disruption amounts to little more than a minor inconvenience. Of course, one would never realize this from the way the Forest Service reacts to a beetle epidemic.

Southern pine beetle control efforts have spawned an entire lexicon of jargon, expenditure of millions of dollars to no avail, and an aura of accomplishment where none exists. It is the epitome of government aggrandizement, a massive self-deception, a bureaucratic program run amuck. In a nutshell, the Forest Service solution to a beetle outbreak is to cut down the healthy trees surrounding the outbreak. In a variant of "feed a fever, starve a cold" (or is it the other way around?), the Forest Service chooses to "feed the sawmill owners, starve the beetles." Fortunately more imaginative control techniques are in the offing. Synthetic pheromones are being developed that draw the male beetles into traps as they pursue their illusory female upwind. Natural enemies are being sought and nurtured in hopes of establishing a more reasonable predator-prey balance. Silvicultural techniques that reduce the hazard of a beetle outbreak are being promoted. But for now the dominant control technique remains the sacrifice of healthy neighboring trees.

First, the Forest Service identifies a spot of beetle-infected trees. Long-infected trees have brown pine needles. Newly infected trees still have green or yellow needles; but small pitch tubes of resin mark the entrance hole where female beetles have penetrated the trunk, and fine bark dust, the result of beetle boring, can be found beneath the hole on the trunk and ground. Then the Forest Service fells infected trees toward the center of the spot. In a buffer zone around the spot, equal in width to the height of the trees (40 to 60 plus feet), uninfected trees are also felled toward the center of the spot. This buffer zone is supposed to interfere with dispersal of the emerging adult beetles and eliminate the source of pheromones. Of course, these beetles do have wings and are quite capable of flying much greater distances (measured in miles) than the width of the buffer strip (measured in feet). Common sense is sometimes uncommon in government programs.

Beetle pupae—that is to say, those undergoing whole body transformation from soft-bodied, wormlike larvae into hard-bodied, winged adults—often remain unaffected by this practice. They may complete their metamorphosis and emerge from the tree trunk for several weeks after the tree is cut. They emerge from logs lying on the ground or, worse, on the logging truck en route to the sawmill, merrily dispersing beetles along the highway. Thus the cut-and-remove control technique can actually help the beetles spread farther afield. Alternatively the felled trees are simply left in place on the ground, where beetles continue to emerge. Fortunately (from an ecological viewpoint) insecticides are not very effective against pine bark beetles and may actually kill more beetle predators than beetles, and for this reason, we have been spared massive aerial spraying programs.

Curiously almost no evidence suggests that these control techniques work. Most infested spots die out without growing larger. Some spots expand considerably. Some treated spots (cut-and-remove or cut-and-leave) die out; others expand considerably. Some spots have been repeatedly cut as many as 27 times before "control" was achieved. The overriding philosophy appears to be "Do something, even if it is wrong (or doesn't work)." Apparently no one in the Forest Service has ever compared the total number of trees lost, including healthy trees sacrificed, in treated spots and untreated spots, to determine if there is any difference. (In 1987, a year of great public controversy regarding pine beetle control, I wrote to the chief of the Forest Service suggesting a simple experimental design that would answer this question. The director of Forest Pest Management responded that the suggestion had been forwarded to the Atlanta regional office, where it apparently died for lack of interest.)

Entrenched bureaucratic procedures gather great momentum. In March 1986 the U.S. House of Representatives Subcommittee on Public Lands of the Committee on Interior and Insular Affairs held a hearing to review the scientific issues related to control of southern pine beetles in the designated southeastern wilderness areas. The Forest Service, in the name of beetle control, had systematically cut infested trees inside and outside wilderness areas, including accumulated buffer cuts as large as 68 to 100 acres at five Texas wilderness areas. It had also harvested approximately 40 percent of the 8,600-acre Kisatchie Hills Wilderness Area in Louisiana, and virtually destroyed 5,600 acres proposed for wilderness designation in east Texas. Public reaction to conversion of wilderness forest to clearcut fields had been strong. A state entomologist from Texas was the principal witness for the Forest Service testifying to the efficacy of the pine beetle control program. Committee members repeatedly inquired about the expert Forest Service employee witnesses. Although there are experts on pine beetles in the Forest Service, none testified before Congress. Numerous academic scientists have concluded that killing the beetles does little to reduce tree mortality and that direct control either does not work or is being improperly applied. No change has been made in the conditions that lead to an outbreak in the first place.

The tragedy becomes absurd when the Forest Service justifies its method of beetle control in the name of protecting the red-cockaded woodpecker. The rationale goes like this. The endangered woodpecker depends on pine trees, particularly old trees, to survive. The old trees are those most susceptible to the pine beetles, particularly cavity trees. Therefore, to save the old trees from the ravages of the pine beetle, the trees must be cut down. Somehow the Forest Service has concluded that the certain death of a tree cut down by a logger is less of a loss to the woodpeckers than the less than certain death of a tree from beetle activity. The beetles seldom kill all the trees in a stand. In most instances they seldom kill even a majority of the trees. Even those trees in a woodpecker colony which are killed have some redeeming value to the birds. They provide a supply of beetles that the woodpeckers can eat. The dead snag will stand for years and provide a suitable nesting site for other woodpecker species, thereby lessening competition for red-cockaded woodpecker cavities. The food and deadwood benefit many other birds and insects that are natural enemies of the beetles. The average beetle infestation is less than 1 acre, while woodpecker territories may exceed 100 acres. All these arguments notwithstanding, the Forest Service believes it has to kill these trees to save them for the woodpeckers.

The Forest Service essentially operates in three arenas: the national forest system, state and private forestry, and research. The research arm gets 5 percent of the total budget and 6 percent of personnel and turns out excellent, high-caliber, statistically sound research, most of which appears to be ignored by the national forest arm. The mass of forest management plans and environmental impact statements generated over the last decade are, to a great extent, devoid of statistical analysis and ecological perspective. Occasionally these documents provide information which disproves their own claims. Such was the case with the environmental impact statement (EIS) for the suppression of the southern pine beetle. The final EIS included some data purporting to prove that beetle control protected woodpecker cavity trees. No statistical analysis was provided. When a simple statistical test was applied to the data, it proved conclusively that there was no difference between woodpecker colonies that had "benefited" from beetle control and other colonies that had been ignored. When informed of the results of this analysis, the Forest Service chose to ignore it.

A final irony exists in the Forest Service program to control pine beetles. Following a large beetle outbreak that kills the majority of the pine trees, the Forest Service prepares the site for replanting. This preparation involves harvesting of all dead and living pines, harvesting or destroying all hardwood trees (which were completely unaffected by the beetles), and windrowing and burning of all forest slash and waste—in other words, total destruction of the remains of the forest. Then a monoculture pine plantation is established. This dense planting of a single pine species that is highly susceptible to beetle attack has, in fact, set the stage for an inevitable future pine beetle epidemic.

Furthermore, a valuable genetic resource is wasted. Sometimes a few large pines are left standing in the midst of the pine beetle destruction. Why have these trees survived? Do they have a genetic resistance to pine beetles? Should they become the breeding stock for our future domesticated "superpines"? No matter. They are cut down with all the dead trees surrounding them. We must wonder again if we are asking the right questions. Do we have too many southern pine beetles? Or do we have too many southern pines?

Woodpeckers as Agents of Biological Control

THERE ARE NO simple solutions to the problems that arise when undesirable plant and animal species compete for the resources of our agricultural ecosystems, including tree farms. By definition, "pests" are simply species growing too well in the "wrong" places—that is to say, places where humans do not want them. Pests can be indigenous, part of the complement of native species found at a given location, or they can be introduced species, transported into a new habitat free of their natural enemies and population control mechanisms. The southern pine beetle is an indigenous pest while house sparrows and starlings are human-transported immigrants that have subsequently prospered in North America and achieved pest status. Many species reach population levels which allow them to be classified as serious pests as a direct result of monocultural farming techniques, as practiced in tree farming.

No single pest control technique is effective under all circumstances. The basic premise of pest control is to reduce the reproductive potential of the pest species. One strategy is to kill breeding or prebreeding individuals, as most pesticides do. Another strategy involves modifying the environment to expose pests to predators, parasites, or damaging environmental conditions. Increasingly, pest control involves sterilization or genetic manipulation of the pest species or development of pest-resistant hosts. Often the job of controlling pests requires a combination of these techniques, or integrated pest management (IPM), to produce the desired result. No aspect of the biological world which potentially affects the lives of pest species can afford to be overlooked.

The predatory role of birds has received little attention from pest control specialists. Although birds are ubiquitous in agroecosystems, they typically escape notice until they become pests in their own right. Though people have long recognized that the presence of birds contributes to the success of agriculture, we have done little to augment their role in the ecosystem. In fact, we have inadvertently done a great deal to diminish their presence by limiting their suitable habitat, seasonal food supply, and nesting requirements. Ounce for ounce, birds have the highest metabolic rates of all animals and daily consume prodigious quantities of food. Nearly all terrestrial birds consume insects at some stage of their life. Even dedicated seedeaters are fed insects during their rapid growth period as nestlings.

Most insectivorous birds are opportunistic or facultative feeders, exploiting a number of prey species when they come across them. Birds adopt a middle-of-the-road approach in selecting their prey, focusing on abundant, palatable species. When different types of prey are available under endemic conditions, birds feed on uncommon species less often than one might expect. Birds typically opt for the most readily available, acceptable prey and overlook the uncommon species. But when a given prey species is extremely abundant, as during an insect epidemic, birds seem to break off feeding on the most available prey and seek out less common species, resulting in a more "balanced" diet. Birds, like people, can become satiated with too much of a good thing.

Can birds really affect insect populations? Birds are, to begin with, at a tremendous reproductive disadvantage. Insects lay eggs by the dozens and hundreds and produce more than one generation per year in some instances. Birds manage a half dozen eggs at best, twice a year for some species, but never give birth to more than a single generation per year, since their offspring require at least a year to mature and produce young of their own. There is no way that birds, or other predators, can keep pace with prolific insects. Under favorable environmental conditions, insect populations, with quick reproduction cycles and short generation times, can burgeon when survivorship is high. Birds, no matter how favorable their natal environment, must survive the ecological crunch of winter before initiating a new generation. During insect outbreaks birds are hopelessly outnumbered. They can eat only so many insects and cannot possibly produce new birds fast enough to take advantage of the abundant food supplies. We are, in fact, witnessing the successful evolutionary strategy of the insects. They concentrate the reproductive adults with attractant pheromones and produce so many offspring, emerging in synchronous pulses, that predators cannot possibly capture them all. This tactic will ensure that enough offspring survive to establish the succeeding generation. When exceptionally favorable conditions coincide, an epidemic occurs.

Observations of avian predation during insect epidemics have fostered a misunderstanding of the potential influence of birds on insect populations. Even when birds each con-

191

sumed 35,000 spruce budworm larvae during an outbreak, they managed to eat no more than 7 percent of the total number of budworms. But to measure the true effectiveness of bird predation on insects, we must examine how much they eat during periods of endemic insect populations between outbreaks. Such studies have shown that birds may consume half to virtually all the insects, even suppressing small outbreaks before they gained momentum.

Some birds specialize in feeding on insect outbreaks. The evening grosbeak is a nomadic species that has a special affinity for spruce budworm outbreaks. Although many species of birds ate budworms during an outbreak in Washington State, the grosbeak was particularly voracious. During the summer, when budworm larvae and pupae were susceptible to predation, the grosbeak population (adults and young) reached 300 birds per square mile at one study location and 1,800 birds per square mile of forest at another. At the lower density, each grosbeak consumed more than 26,000 budworms during the 55-day period of availability. The grosbeaks ate nearly 8 million budworms per square mile, 43 percent of all bird predation. At the site with higher grosbeak density, each bird consumed more than 12,000 budworms, or 23 million budworms per square mile of forest and 70 percent of total bird predation. Each grosbeak was the functional equivalent of $6.80 and $1.80, respectively, of insecticide application. Over a one hundred year harvest cycle, the Douglas fir-ponderosa pine forest provides $518,000 of forest products, and its birds provide pest control equivalent to $118,000 in spraying costs, both expressed as net present value per square mile. Such savings should certainly draw the attention of budget-conscious forest managers. Historically, budworm outbreaks have appeared about every 28 years in this region. Without the assistance of birds, outbreaks might occur every 3 years.

This important study demonstrated that some bird species can exert substantial pressure on insect populations, particularly during low-density, endemic years. But grosbeaks glean budworms and similar insect forms from growing needles. While woodpeckers join the assemblage of birds feeding on such critters during outbreaks, do their normal foraging habits have a similar effect on other pests?

A number of studies have demonstrated that woodpeckers are very valuable to agroecosystems, especially cornfields. Corn plants are ideal crops for studying the impact of woodpeckers. The cornstalk serves as a surrogate tree, and bird attacks on the ears of corn or standing stalks are readily detectable and quantifiable.

Flickers are capable of removing 78 percent of overwintering corn borers. In experiments, researchers screened birds from some rows of corn, and 29 percent of the plants became infested with corn borers. In adjacent rows, where flickers had free access, infestation rates dropped from 32 to only 2 percent after five months. In another study flickers removed 64 and 82 percent of corn borer larvae in two different years, and 68 and 60 percent of larvae in a statewide survey of Mississippi in the same years.

Hairy woodpeckers prey on earworms in cornfields. One study examined 1,000 years of corn and found that earworms had infested 96 percent of them. The woodpeckers missed only 249 ears containing earworm larvae and removed larvae from 677 ears. The birds bypassed all the uninfested ears, and in 35 percent of the total crop they removed the larvae before kernel damage occurred. Woodpeckers have removed 34 to 63 percent of overwintering codling moths in apple orchards. Woodpecker predation alone reduced moth populations to a tolerable level in 74 percent of the orchards studied.

Insect predators and insect parasites may be competing for the same prey resource as woodpeckers and other birds. It is possible that an increase in avian predation on a parasite may result in a decrease in the total predatory pressure, from birds plus parasites, on a host insect species. This would favor, rather than inhibit, pest population growth. For birds to help limit the numbers of a target pest species, they must consume a portion of the target population that insect predators or parasites would not normally kill. If only a small proportion of the target population carries parasites, additional predation by birds will limit population growth. If a large percentage of the target species has been parasitized, additional bird predation would contribute little to controlling the population.

Codling moths in the larval stage and carrying braconid insect parasites are smaller than unparasitized larvae and often elude detection by woodpeckers. Only 3 percent of larvae captured by woodpeckers had parasites, whereas 14 percent of the larvae they passed up did. Here clearly the actions of the avian predator and a parasite are complementary, in terms of their combined effect on the target species. The woodpeckers removed an average of 52 percent of the codling moth larvae over a seven-year period and thus appear to be far more effective in controlling the moths than the parasites.

A study of woodpecker predation on insect borers in hardwood forests found that the birds removed 39 percent of white oak borers, 39 percent of living beech borers, and 13 or 65 percent of poplar borers on two stands. Forest management practices seem to affect predation rates. In 12-year-old trees regenerating a clearcut, woodpeckers consumed only 7 and 13 percent of second-year red oak borers on two sites. However, only half as many downy and hairy woodpeckers lived in this dense regenerating vegetation, which lacked large trees, as in surrounding uncut woodlands.

Elsewhere three species of woodpeckers reduced populations of the Engelmann spruce beetle (*Dendroctonus engelmanni*), a close relative of the southern pine beetle, by 45 to 98 percent. Woodpeckers may kill more southern pine beetles than any other force in nature. In east Texas six species of woodpeckers inhabited the pine and pine-hardwood forests experiencing a beetle outbreak. Three species—red-bellied woodpecker, common flicker, and yellow-bellied sapsucker— did more than three-quarters of their foraging in hardwood trees and uninfested pines. The remaining species—downy, hairy, and pileated woodpeckers—did 80 percent or more of their foraging in infested pine trees.

A number of pine trees were screened to exclude woodpeckers, while other trees permitted free woodpecker predation. Beetles in the egg and early larval stages are extremely small and live entirely within cambium tissue beneath the bark. They are difficult to detect and inefficient to excavate, providing a meager reward for a lot of work. Consequently the researchers detected no difference in larval density between unscreened and screened pine trees. The larger beetle pupae, which bore outward into the bark, appeared easier to detect and more worth the effort, as screened trees, which prevented woodpecker predation, had pupal densities 15 times greater than unscreened trees. The woodpeckers also killed additional beetles indirectly. As the birds flaked off pine bark, they exposed beetle tunnels to the external environment. Unprotected by the insulating bark, the larvae soon withered or were eaten by brown creepers and black-and-white warblers. Fungi invaded the open beetle galleries, killing the larvae deeper within. Even the pieces of bark broken loose by the woodpeckers added to beetle losses, as 80 percent of the beetles in the bark failed to emerge.

The woodpeckers responded to southern pine beetle infestations in two ways. First, several species changed their foraging behavior. Before the infestation, woodpeckers foraged in hardwood trees of several species or in pine trees. Figure 10-1, p. 198, depicts the woodpeckers' increased preference for pine trees during the infestation. Downy woodpeckers doubled their frequency of foraging in pine trees when they encountered the beetle infestations. Hairy woodpeckers, which conducted three-fourths of their foraging in pine trees in the absence of a beetle infestation, shifted to foraging in pines almost exclusively. Pileated woodpeckers increased their pine foraging 50 percent. In contrast, the omnivorous red-bellied woodpeckers actually decreased the proportion of pines

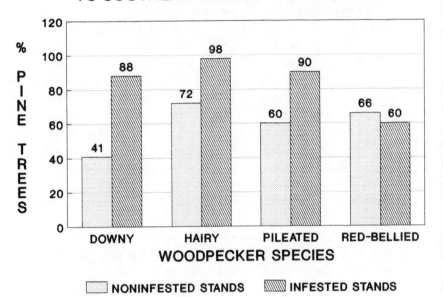

FIGURE 10-1 The response of woodpeckers to outbreaks of southern pine beetles.

among trees they foraged. Thus three woodpecker species responded positively to increased availability of southern pine beetles as prey while the fourth species did not respond.

There was a second reaction to the beetles. Downy, hairy, and pileated woodpeckers became 8 to 58 times more abundant, during various months of the year, within beetle-infested timber stands as compared with noninfested stands. The densities of red-bellied woodpeckers also increased, but only by 3 to 20 times. Thus beetle infestation attracted woodpeckers from the surrounding forest. This was probably accompanied by a relaxation of territorial defenses, a common occurrence when resources become so abundant that it is not expedient to waste energy in defending them.

In summary, birds in general, and woodpeckers in particular, exhibit several characteristics that make them good biological control agents. Woodpeckers are adaptable to different environments and changing conditions, as demonstrated by their flexible foraging patterns and broad range of habitats. Ranging over large territories, woodpeckers can search extensive areas, improving the probability that they will encounter areas of high pest density or incipient outbreaks. Woodpeckers also feed on many different prey and can survive in areas without high concentrations of any particular insect. They are thus able to lessen or prevent outbreaks more readily than insect predators and parasites, which tend to be very host-specific. As environmental temperatures decline, the growth and development of the overwintering generation of insects slow, permitting woodpeckers to feed on a single generation of insects for a longer period of time. During this same winter period of scarce food, woodpeckers concentrate more of their foraging attention on insects buried in tree trunks and limbs. Because they fail to match the reproductive potential of their insect prey, woodpeckers cannot begin to cope with an burgeoning insect population. Woodpecker predation, therefore, becomes a crucial force at endemic levels of insect pests, contributes to limiting epidemic insect densities (excessively prevalent), but is ineffectual in controlling insect populations under pandemic (outbreak) conditions.

To this point we have said nothing about red-cockaded woodpeckers and insect control. When a given species has become so rare as to be officially recognized as endangered, it also becomes difficult to proclaim that it plays a vital role in insect control. In fact, its role has not even been studied. But it is interesting to speculate. We have a particular pest, the southern pine beetle, that specializes in pine trees. Although we know that pine beetle epidemics occurred during colonial times, the interval between outbreaks appears to have shortened dramatically in recent decades, and the geographic extent of individual outbreaks seems to have broadened. We also have the ultimate pinewoods specialist, the red-cockaded woodpecker, which forages predominantly on pine trunks. It scales off pieces of pine bark that are likely to reveal emerging adult beetles, which woodpeckers and other tree trunk foragers eat. The thinner bark leads to increased solar heating and desiccation, the exposed galleries permit entry of fungi harmful to the beetles, and the survival of beetles in bark chips which fall to the ground becomes far less likely.

The beetle, the woodpecker, and the pines all evolved together; they have proved that they are capable of coexistence. When humans ravaged the pine forests at the turn of the century, the beetle and the woodpecker both lost their most valuable resource—old pine trees. Only pines larger than 12 to 14 inches diameter were harvested, but virtually all these were cut. The beetle and the woodpecker survived this major change in their environment, and the forests regrew. But the new forest was different from the old. The trees were, in silvicultural jargon, overstocked. As these densely packed pine trees grew older, ideal conditions for the beetle developed. With their great reproductive potential, beetle populations take advantage of favorable environmental conditions and reach epidemic densities. Meanwhile, clearcutting harvests and pine beetle control efforts fragment the forest, continually degrading woodpecker habitat. With an inherently low reproductive potential, evolved during more hospitable times, the woodpecker is unable to keep pace and populations steadily shrink.

It is curious that populations of a natural predator of pine beetles, the red-cockaded woodpecker, declined at the same time that beetle epidemics became more frequent and widespread. Are they possibly connected? This scenario, although logical, is purely speculative. It is worth considering as we seek explanations for the natural phenomena—extinction and outbreak—that surround us.

Peckerwood Politics

PROTECTION FOR ENDANGERED species has evolved in fits and starts. Congress in 1966 passed the Endangered Species Preservation Act, which required federal agencies to protect native forms of wildlife threatened with extinction. This law lacked enforcement authority and was replaced in 1969 by the Endangered Species Conservation Act. The 1969 act increased funds for habitat acquisition, made it a crime to import or export any member of a designated endangered species, and extended protection to species worldwide. But species had to be on the verge of extinction to be listed as endangered, no one was prohibited from taking an endangered animal, and stable but jeopardized populations were not protected.

Congress finally put teeth into the rhetoric by passing the Endangered Species Act of 1973. This legislation created two categories of protection—endangered species and threatened species—opened protection to all animals and plants, made it a crime to violate regulations designed to protect designated species, required all federal agencies to conserve endangered wildlife, and provided for the listing of critical habitats, defined as areas essential to the survival of listed species. Although hunting has decimated some species, most extinctions caused by humans are the result of habitat destruction. For this reason, designation of critical habitat often becomes a central feature of protection.

The designation of species as endangered or threatened has always been an excruciatingly slow process, but listing virtually halted when the Reagan administration began requiring the Fish and Wildlife Service to consider economic impacts in the listing procedures. In 1982 Congress amended the Endangered Species Act to clarify that listing decisions were to depend solely on scientific and commercial data. Economic impacts could come into play only when the designation of critical habitat was being considered.

The Endangered Species Act identified the U.S. Fish and Wildlife Service as the lead federal agency in charge of protecting and conserving officially designated (by the secretary of the interior or the secretary of commerce) threatened and endangered species of plants and wildlife (except marine species). The act requires the U.S. Fish and Wildlife Service to designate "recovery teams" of responsible officials and experts to develop "recovery plans" that would guide the conservation and survival of populations of threatened and endangered species. The ultimate goal of each recovery team was to increase the population of the designated species to the point where it could be delisted and the team could be dissolved.

The American Ornithologists' Union (AOU) Committee on Conservation independently evaluated the progress of the recovery team concept in 1977 by reviewing the activity of nineteen recovery teams developing recovery plans for birds, including the red-cockaded woodpecker team. The AOU committee found that although the recovery teams were directed to consider only biological information during the preparation of their recovery plans, socioeconomic and political considerations often determined significantly the shape of the final plan adopted. The committee report noted a number of strengths and weaknesses in the recovery team concept and proffered a number of recommendations, including increased emphasis on biological, rather than political or socioeconomic, considerations. The committee concluded that the recovery team and recovery plan concept had made a substantial contribution to the conservation of endangered species, with some species benefiting more than others.

The red-cockaded woodpecker first gained endangered species status in 1968. The Fish and Wildlife Service sponsored a symposium to pull together existing information on the species in May 1971. The U.S. Forest Service initiated work on management guidelines in 1972 but did not complete and issue them until 1975. The guidelines recommended that 40 acres of pines 20 or more years of age be maintained, under even-aged silvicultural management, adjacent to woodpecker colonies. Harvest rotations were set at 80 years for longleaf pine and 70 years for other species. Within the colony buffer area, the basal area (cumulative cross-sectional area of tree trunks) of pines was to be kept within 50 to 80 square feet per acre.

In June 1975 the Fish and Wildlife Service appointed a 5-member recovery team to draft a Recovery Plan for the red-cockaded woodpecker. The sensitive political nature of the handling of this species was apparent from the onset. The makeup of the team was rather curious. It included 2 experienced researchers familiar with the species, 1 from a private research organization and the other, the team leader, from a large university. A wildlife specialist from the Forest Service, with considerable knowledge of the species, was also appointed. A forester from the Fish and Wildlife Service and a wildlife biologist from an industrial forest corporation, neither of whom had particularly thorough knowledge of the species, rounded out the team, Thus, initially, only 3 of the 5 team members had any experience with the bird, while 2 of the members, plus the Fish and Wildlife Service liaison representative, did not consider the species actually endangered. The stage for confrontation was set, and forest industry interests were well entrenched.

The team leader, Jerry Jackson, gradually added knowledgeable consultants to the group: an expert from Texas, two Forest Service researchers, a university researcher, and an informed observer. These additions gave the group geographic balance, with collective field experience from Texas, Louisiana, Mississippi, and South Carolina. The Forest Service retained its heavy influence. The recovery team held its first meeting in November 1975. The first draft of a Recovery Plan was due in June 1976.

Controversial issues dominated the meetings from the start. What criteria could the team use to determine when the species was no longer endangered so that it could be removed from the endangered species list? Could stable populations, such as that on the Francis Marion National Forest in South Carolina, be removed from the list? What was the impact of even-aged forest management? How big could clearcut harvests be? How long should forest rotation periods be? How should recommended management practices be implemented and evaluated? Forest management practices and removal of the species from endangered status dominated discussions then, and still do now, 15 years and many fewer birds later.

A pattern quickly emerged. The team leader drafted sections of the Recovery Plan. The team and consultants discussed each issue and revised the text at each team meeting.

The meetings were held at a new location each time, and the group visited woodpecker colonies at each site to understand geographical variation in site requirements. The team met in South Carolina, Mississippi, Texas, Florida, and Georgia.

Discussions regarding the impact of forest management practices on the woodpecker were protracted and divisive and failed to produce consensus. The recovery plan took shape slowly. The team submitted its first draft in July 1976 to the Fish and Wildlife Service, which disseminated it widely for comment. The plan recommended such forest management practices as designating the woodpecker as the featured species for habitat management, maintaining 100 acres of contiguous pine forest 40 years of age or older for each colony, using 100-year harvest rotations for longleaf pine and 80-year rotations for other pine species, and preserving a basal area of 50 to 80 square feet per acre in colonies.

Reviewers' comments fell along predictable lines. Organizations and agencies oriented toward timber production objected to the large acreage and longer rotations. University biologists recommended even larger acreage (200 acres) and longer rotations (130 and 110 years). Unsurprisingly the Forest Service, which manages harvest within the national forests, had the strongest objections and requested an opportunity to present its case to the recovery team.

The team met in January 1977 to respond to reviewer comments and the Forest Service. A Forest Service wildlife biologist presented a highly choreographed case in support of existing management policy, to the point of asking the team members to agree with each individual point as he led them through the presentation. Rather than 100 acres of pines 40 years or older to support each woodpecker colony, the Forest Service wanted to retain its existing guideline: 40 acres of pines 20 or more years of age. The service urged that rotation lengths remain at 80 years for longleaf and 70 years for other pine species, arguing that the woodpeckers had ample time to select new cavity trees before they were harvested (tantamount to a "use it or lose it" philosophy). The service also insisted that home range requirements be set according to the size of home ranges in woodpecker-saturated habitats, where clans lived closely surrounded by other clans and territory expansion was prohibited. This approach would, of course, yield useful information on the minimum territory required in good habitats but would not address territory requirements in poor habitats typical over the birds' entire range.

Finally, the Forest Service, noting the team's disunity regarding even-aged forest management, insisted that the large number of woodpeckers on national forests—85 percent of the woodpeckers on only 5 percent of available commercial forestland—demonstrated that even-aged management was not only compatible but the best management strategy for woodpecker survival. As a footnote the Forest Service requested that a recommendation on critical habitat be postponed until after the recovery plan was completed.

The team fell into complete disarray at this meeting in Macon, Georgia. Some participants interpreted parts of the Forest Service presentation as a thinly veiled assault on the team leader. Infighting based on the economic consequences of longer rotations and larger support stands erupted. As the second day of the meeting began, the regional director of the Fish and Wildlife Service, hurriedly called in from Atlanta, quelled the disruption as he reestablished the biological orientation of the recovery plan as preeminent. But consensus was difficult to achieve. The functional role of the consultants came into question, as forestry interests insisted that consultants should not have a vote on disputed issues. Earlier the Fish and Wildlife Service had indicated its willingness to add one or more of the consultants as full team members, but when requested to do so, the service refused to take action.

On May 17, 1977, the Fish and Wildlife Service rendered its Biological Opinion regarding red-cockaded woodpecker management on national forests in Texas. The service insisted on 100 acres of pines 60 or more years of age contiguous with each colony. Harvest rotations were to be extended to 100 years for longleaf and shortleaf pines and 80 years for loblolly pines if field studies indicated that the woodpeckers did not start moving into and establishing new colonies in 60-year-old pine stands. Since the report's issue no new colonies have been established in Texas.

The next two drafts of the plan (September and November 1977) retained the 100- and 80-year rotations. The support stand requirement expanded to 200 acres, but the age recommendation was dropped. This situation soon changed. By the time the team met for final approval the management recommendation had regressed to 100 acres 40 or more years of age. As an indication of its significance, the 2 pages of management recommendations had more revisions than all the other 23 pages of text combined. After all the shots were fired and the smoke had cleared, the final recommendations called for 200 acres of contiguous pine forest without an age stipulation. The long battle had concluded, but the war had apparently just begun. The Recovery Plan languished deep in the bowels of the Fish and Wildlife Service for many months, finally emerging in August 1979.

Unresolved was the issue of critical habitat. In January 1977 the recovery team and consultants held extended discussions regarding critical habitat. Only one, the Fish and Wildlife Service team member, voted against designating critical habitat for the species. A colony site was defined as the aggregate of colony trees plus a 200-foot buffer zone around the aggregate. A support stand was defined as a minimum of 40 acres of pine forest 60 or more years of age adjacent to the colony site. Critical habitat was defined as a minimum of 200 acres of pine forest (50 to 100 percent pine trees) containing or contiguous to the colony site and support stand. Critical habitat exists in Texas, Louisiana, Arkansas, Oklahoma, Mississippi, Tennessee, Kentucky, Alabama, Georgia, Florida, South Carolina, North Carolina, Virginia, Maryland, and possibly southern Missouri.

The regional director of the Fish and Wildlife Service forwarded the team's recommendation for critical habitat to Washington but recommended against its adoption. The regional office thought that designation of critical habitat would require that each colony site and its surrounding 200 acres be mapped, action it considered impractical, if not impossible. The regional office argued that while a particular site may be critical to an individual bird or individual colony, it would not be critical to survival of the species as a whole.

The recovery team leader, Jerome Jackson, responded by pointing out that loss of habitat was the primary reason the woodpecker was endangered. Loss of a single colony would further jeopardize the continued existence of the species because it would reduce the gene pool and further fragment the species' populations. Since habitat loss was the greatest cause of the species' endangered status, the Fish and Wildlife Service should designate areas of critical habitat and give them special management consideration.

Critical habitat has never been designated for the red-cockaded woodpecker. Recovery teams are supposed to function until the species recovers and can be removed from the endangered species list. The red-cockaded woodpecker recovery team was disbanded in 1982.

Research on the red-cockaded woodpecker increased as interest and available funds swelled. The U.S. Forest Service initiated a major research program on the Francis Marion National Forest in South Carolina. A second symposium was held in 1983. In addition to the proceedings of the two symposia, nearly 100 technical papers on the red-cockaded woodpecker were published between 1970 and 1983.

In 1980 the U.S. Fish and Wildlife Service issued a Biological Opinion regarding the Forest Service timber harvest plans for the southeastern United States, finding that these harvest plans would jeopardize the woodpecker. The Biological Opinion offered two alternatives. The Forest Service could either (1) extend the harvest rotation age to 100 plus years for longleaf pine and 80 plus years for other pines or (2) offset shorter rotations of 80 plus years for longleaf and 70 plus years for other pines with the establishment of 25-acre recruitment stands of old-growth pines as future colony sites, with one recruitment stand within one-quarter to three-quarters of a mile of each colony.

Since extension of rotations was anathema to the Forest Service, it naturally favored the second alternative. But swelling scientific consensus viewed that tactic as inadequate to preserve the species. Consequently, in 1984 the National Wildlife Federation filed a notice of violation of the Endangered Species Act with the Fish and Wildlife Service and the Forest Service. The two services subsequently agreed to formal consultation to develop new management guidelines, which were issued in 1985.

Concurrently, since the recovery team had been disbanded in 1982, the Fish and Wildlife Service contracted with the Forest Service to develop revisions to the team's Recovery Plan. Michael Lennartz, project leader of the Forest Service research effort on the Francis Marion National Forest, was selected to revise the Recovery Plan. There is no question that Lennartz's knowledge and experience ranked him among the top woodpecker biologists in the nation. He had served as a consultant to the recovery team itself. However, as a career Forest Service employee he would come under intense pressure to develop revisions that the service could live with, a clear conflict of interest.

The revision, released in 1985, was so extensive as to amount to an entirely new Recovery Plan. It added some important new features, deleted some provisions of the 1979 plan, and included some controversial elements. A major contribution concerned the definition of foraging habitat. Recall the controversy over appropriate acreage (40 versus 100 or 200 acres) and age (20 or 40 or 60 years) of forest adjacent to each colony. The second Recovery Plan defined "well-stocked" habitat as 60 or more square feet of basal area per acre, with 50 percent or more of the basal area as pine trees, 30 or more years old, with at least 24 pine trees 10 inches or more in diameter per acre. At least 125 acres of such habitat, with 40 percent (50 acres) of the acreage 60 or more years old, should be contiguous with each colony.

This definition went a long way toward providing good woodpecker habitat, but were 125 acres enough? The Forest Service research on the Francis Marion National Forest, prime woodpecker habitat, had determined that the average amount of good foraging habitat for 17 woodpecker clans constrained by adjacent territories was 126 acres. This meant that being the average, 126 acres would accommodate approximately one-half of the woodpecker clans. The other half required more acreage, as much as 400 plus acres. Clearly 125 acres would not suffice.

The plan also addressed the issue of what to do in poor habitat. The 125 acres of preferred foraging habitat contained an average of 21,250 pine stems with a total basal area of 8,490 square feet and 6,350 pine stems 10 inches or more in diameter. In younger habitat, with trees of smaller diameter, or in sparsely stocked habitat, forest managers should provide enough acreage to supply as many large trees as the average preferred foraging habitat. The danger lay in the tendency for managers simply to provide 125 acres, which is easily determined, without guaranteeing the second component, number and size of trees, which is more difficult to ascertain.

The plan made important recommendations regarding colony management. Potential cavity trees were defined as longleaf pines 95 or more years old or other pines 75 or more years old. Hardwood trees were to be kept below 20 square feet per acre basal area and all hardwoods greater than 1 inch in diameter within 50 feet of a cavity tree were to be removed. A distance of 20 to 25 feet should be maintained between pine trees to minimize pine beetle infestations. All these changes would certainly help the woodpecker.

The revised plan did not mention the Forest Service buga-
boo, harvest rotation ages, but it did plow new ground with
another Forest Service favorite, delisting of the red-cockaded
woodpecker as an endangered species. The Endangered Species Act specified that Recovery Plans should include objective, measurable criteria which, when met, would result in a
determination that the species be removed from the list of
endangered species. The Forest Service had been pushing for
delisting of the red-cockaded woodpecker for many years.

The revised Recovery Plan specified that a population
larger than 250 clans would be considered "recovered" when
supported by an adequate habitat management program. The
existence of 15 viable populations with a specific geographic
distribution across the bird's range would permit the species
to be delisted. The existence of 6 viable populations with a
specific geographic distribution would allow downlisting to
"threatened" status. The bird would be considered "endangered" only when no viable populations existed in one or
more defined areas: the coastal plain of North or South Carolina, the sandhill region of North or South Carolina, the
coastal plain of Georgia or peninsular Florida, the coastal
plain of Alabama or the Florida panhandle, the coastal plain
of Mississippi, or the coastal plain of Louisiana or Texas.

Since the forest management plan, written by the Forest
Service, and the woodpecker management plan, written for
the Fish and Wildlife Service by a Forest Service employee,
were produced simultaneously, the Fish and Wildlife Service
accepted the new Recovery Plan and found that the new forest guidelines did not jeopardize the woodpecker. The rest of
the world was not so complacent. The International Council
for Bird Preservation asked the American Ornithologists'
Union to appoint an investigative committee. The committee
was formed in late 1983 and charged with reviewing the status
of the woodpecker, evaluating the conservation and management practices impinging on its welfare, and furthering the
interest of the AOU in providing scientific advice and sugges-

tions to managers of threatened and endangered species. The committee issued its report in October 1986.

It determined that the red-cockaded woodpecker had become endangered because of its dependence on mature, open pine woodlands. This fire-dependent habitat had become very scarce as a result of timber harvest and fire exclusion. Forest management practices which produced and harvested only young trees on private land and middle-aged trees on public land threatened the continued existence of the species. Further woodpecker population decline could probably be prevented by maintenance of suitable habitat.

The committee concluded that conservation of the woodpecker would require multiple approaches, including accurate population censuses, enforcement of legally mandated management procedures, experimental studies of the production of cavity trees, designation of at least one national forest primarily for studies of the woodpeckers, evaluation of the 1985 Recovery Plan recommendations for foraging habitat in different geographic regions, and evaluation of the replacement/ recruitment stand concept. The committee noted that after 15 years of protection as an endangered species, the species continued to decline and local extirpations had been numerous. The timber industry perceived the species as a serious economic burden, and no management program had led to increased numbers of the birds.

The AOU committee specifically addressed five facets of the revised Recovery Plan. It questioned the adequacy of the recommended 125 acres of foraging habitat per clan because 125 acres represented breeding season territory rather than year-round home range requirements (215 acres at the same site, the Francis Marion National Forest). Moreover, this acreage might well be insufficient on poor habitat, and the committee thought that recommendations for endangered species should risk error on the side of conservation, especially when many variables influence habitat quality.

The committee questioned the adequacy of 30-year-old

pine trees as foraging habitat, noting a design fault in the study which led to the recommendation that 60 percent of the 125 acres (75 acres) should be 30 or more years of age. It noted that accurate censuses of all populations were essential to determining the current status of the bird. It estimated that attainment of 1 clan per 200 to 400 acres of national forest land should be sufficient to safeguard the species. The committee correctly surmised that the $5.5 million recommended for 3 years of recovery activity was unlikely to materialize.

Addressing the issue of minimum viable populations, set at 250 clans or 500 birds, the committee noted that downgrading to threatened status could occur with only 6 populations or 3,000 birds, or fewer than were believed to exist at that time. Delisting could occur with 15 populations of 500 birds, or 7,500 total, again perhaps fewer than the total alive at that time. The committee noted that 500 breeding birds did not equal an effective population of 500 because some proportion of the birds would be unsuccessful in nesting. It concluded that designation of such an untested minimal value as representing a viable population was unjustified. It also expressed concern that emphasis on 15 large populations might lead forest managers to conclude that small but connecting populations were not critical.

To overcome these shortcomings in the revised Recovery Plan, the committee made a number of recommendations. Foremost was the initiation of programs specifically to increase the number of woodpeckers. The committee noted that current management practices were inadequate for recovery of the species and that most national forests had fallen short of existing legal requirements. It recommended that harvest rotations be extended to 80 or more years and that large tracts of old-growth forest be developed. Timber management should foster suppression of tree growth in dense stands and subsequent release by harvest to produce more potential cavity trees. The committee urged that all trees, rather than just 40 percent of them, in the 125 acres of forag-

211

ing habitat should be 60 or more years old. It noted that 10 acres of 60-year-old trees were probably insufficient as a recruitment stand, and there was no evidence that the birds would colonize isolated habitats. It urged that connecting habitat corridors be established to counteract increasing fragmentation and isolation of populations. Relocation of birds should be attempted only under extreme circumstances.

The Fish and Wildlife Service and the Forest Service have ignored the AOU committee recommendations. The recommendations highlighted the most critical weakness of the revised Recovery Plan, which emphasized a minimal strategy. The plan recommended the minimal area (125 acres) of foraging habitat to sustain a clan of birds. It recommended the minimal age (30 years) of trees and the minimal proportion (40 percent) of older trees in the foraging habitat. It established a minimal number of birds (500) as a viable population and a minimal number of populations to change the bird's protective status—6 for downlisting to "threatened" and 15 for delisting altogether. Minimum provisions allow absolutely no room for error or miscalculation. "Minimalism" is a dangerous strategy to employ when one is trying to rescue a declining species.

Meanwhile,
Deep in the
Heart of Texas . . .

TWO FOREST SERVICE wildlife biologists at the Wildlife Habitat and Silviculture Laboratory of the Southern Forest Experiment Station at Nacogdoches, Texas, made a startling discovery. Richard Conner and Craig Rudolph had been studying red-cockaded woodpeckers in the Angelina National Forest. This 150,000-acre forest, split in two by the Sam Rayburn Reservoir, harbors two disjunct woodpecker populations. One population inhabits stands of loblolly and shortleaf pine; the other lies 20 miles away in a longleaf pine forest. All of the red-cockaded woodpecker cavity and start hole trees in the forest had been located, tagged, and mapped. Conner and Rudolph categorized each tree as actively used by the wood-

213

peckers or abandoned, and they determined the number of birds in the clan at each colony.

This last step was the critical one. The Forest Service had been locating and mapping woodpecker colonies for years and classifying them as either active or inactive. This is a comparatively simple task, though prone to error. If no birds were observed, as most frequently happened, activity was determined by the presence of fresh resin oozing from around the cavity entrance entrance or resin wells. However, fresh resin can also come from pileated woodpeckers foraging for grubs or enlarging cavities, or yellow-bellied sapsuckers creating sap wells, or even burrowing beetles. Verifying the actual presence of red-cockaded woodpeckers requires that researchers go that extra mile, actually many extra miles, and visit the colonies at dawn and dusk, when the woodpeckers are first emerging or are coming back to roost. This work means long days afield, getting to the colony before daylight and leaving the forest after dark. But nothing else will suffice to determine the actual status of a given colony.

The diligence of Conner and Rudolph revealed that although 38 of the 62 red-cockaded colonies in the Angelina National Forest were active in 1983, only 22 colonies (35 percent) remained active in 1987. Furthermore, clans of woodpeckers were virtually nonexistent. Of the colonies, 4 colonies had 3 birds in the clan, the breeding pair plus 1 helper, 11 colonies were occupied by just a pair of birds, and 7 colonies had only 1 bird present. A single-bird "clan" is 1 male clinging tenaciously to his "inherited" territory and is doomed to extinction unless a young female appears to join him. Only 14 of the colonies were producing young birds, and there were only 47 woodpeckers alive in the two populations combined.

Alarmed by what their research was revealing, Conner and Rudolph expanded their studies to the nearby Sabine and Davy Crockett national forests. These two forests, lying east and west of the Angelina National Forest, are similar in size, about 160,000 acres each, but have more hardwood vegetation mixed with the pine trees. The findings on these forests were even more distressing. Only 27 of the 134 colonies (20 percent) in the Davy Crockett National Forest were active, with 52 birds remaining. In the Sabine National Forest only 6 of the 62 colonies (10 percent) were active, with a total of 12 birds. Only 9 colonies in the Davy Crockett, and 3 in the Sabine, produced young birds during 1987.

Clearly a crisis threshold had been breached. Five consecutive years of census data for the period 1983–1987 demonstrated an annual loss of 10.5 percent of active colonies in the Angelina National Forest, or 42 percent over the 5-year period. Should this trend continue, active colonies would disappear by 1993 (see Figure 12-1, p. 218). Information from four surveys of the Davy Crockett National Forest told a similar story. Active colonies had declined 57 percent between 1981 and 1987 and were likely to disappear by 1992. Nationally recognized as a woodpecker expert, Conner took his indisputable data to administrators of the Forest Service. With only 113 red-cockaded woodpeckers dispersed in 56 active colonies in these three national forests, and populations declining at 8.4 to 14.5 percent annually, there was little time to lose.

Such a precipitous decline was not unprecedented. The harbinger had been a study, coordinated by Richard Thompson, that surveyed 312 colonies known to be active in 1969 and 1970 in 10 states. When reexamined in 1973 and 1974, only 271 were still active, a 13 percent loss in 4 years. This study was discounted by officialdom because it did not consider the possibility that the woodpeckers had moved to new colonies.

My own studies on the 200,000-acre Savannah River Plant National Environmental Research Park (SRP NERP) in South Carolina exposed the same trend. The Forest Service had located 12 active and 3 abandoned colonies from 1969 to 1974. In 1975 the Forest Service, Joe Skorupa, and I at-

ACTIVE COLONY TRENDS ON
NATIONAL FORESTS IN TEXAS

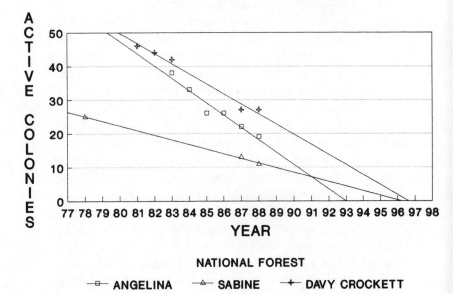

FIGURE 12-1 The decline of red-cockaded woodpecker colonies on three national forests in Texas.

tempted to re-locate these colonies and identify new ones. Only 5 of the 12 active colonies remained active; 3 had been abandoned, and 4 we could not find at all, apparently because of cavity tree fall or removal. We found 7 additional colonies, 5 of them active. In 1976 we located 4 additional active colonies, bringing the known number of colonies on the SRP NERP to 26. The results were not encouraging.

We found the colonies grouped in 4 clusters plus several isolated sites. All 6 colonies in 1 cluster were abandoned. A cluster of 4 colonies, and another of 6, were active. The fourth cluster was in transition. In addition, 1 colony site had disappeared, 2 had been abandoned, and another was abandoned during our 2-year survey, declining from 2 birds in 1975 to 1 in 1976 and finally to none by January 1977. Another colony consisted of a single bird in 1975, which acquired a mate but raised no young in 1976, declined to a single bird once more in 1977, and disappeared soon after. The sixth colony appeared promising, with 3 birds present in 1975 but only 1 bird in 1976 and 1977, and that one soon vanished. The hope offered by the two clumps of active colonies also proved illusory. By 1984 only 2 nesting pairs and 6 lone males remained; by 1987 other researchers could find only 3 solitary males.

We had captured and color-banded some of these woodpeckers to permit recognition, using binoculars, of individual birds in the forest. During the summer of 1975, 9 birds were banded but 2 could not be located the following winter. During the summer of 1976, 20 banded adults were alive and well, but 6 of them had disappeared by winter. Ornithologists have come to expect heavy losses of juvenile birds of all species, but only prolific breeding can overcome 22 to 30 percent annual losses of adults. Red-cockaded woodpeckers, with only 1 female per clan and 1 clutch of eggs per year, are not prolific under the best of conditions.

The best-documented decline of red-cockaded woodpeckers tracked the 12 clans on the 2,800-acre Tall Timbers Research Station in northern Florida. From 30 adults in 1968 the population peaked at 40 birds and 11 nests in 1970, plunged to 24 birds the following year and 16 by 1974. After a modest increase to 19 birds in 1975, the population steadily declined to 10 birds scattered in 6 clans, 2 with a single bird each, by 1980, when only one nesting attempt was made. The last woodpecker was seen alive in 1981.

These three episodes demonstrated rapid population decline in three distinct areas of the species' range: Texas, Florida, and South Carolina. While forest management practices seemed to have caused the decline in Texas and South Carolina, the extirpation of the birds at Tall Timbers is the most perplexing. It is a research site. No timber was cut, and no dead trees were salvaged. No pesticides or herbicides were used. The forest was burned annually, and an open, parklike habitat was maintained. The pine trees averaged 85 years old when the study began and thus were 100 years old when extirpation occurred. The nearest off-site colony was only 3 miles away, and a concentration of colonies was 6 miles distant, well within the dispersal range of the species. If there was ever a forest where red-cockadeds should have persisted, Tall Timbers was it. But they disappeared. The forest stands as a sobering monument to woodpecker biologists who think they understand the environmental requirements of this species.

While we admit that we may not understand all that we know about red-cockaded woodpecker biology, conservation efforts must press on. The 1973 Forest and Rangeland Renewable Resources Planning Act and the 1976 National Forest Management Act directed the Forest Service to establish a long-term planning process to ensure multiple use and sustained yield of the public forests. The national forests were established for outdoor recreation, range, timber, watershed, and wildlife and fish purposes. Congress has defined multiple use as the harmonious and coordinated management of the various resources, each with the other, without impairing the productivity of the land. Multiple use requires that consideration be given to the relative values of the various resources, not necessarily the combination of uses that will provide the greatest dollar return or the greatest unit output.

Each national forest has developed a 50-year plan, considering a number of alternative management schemes, to comply best with the multiple-use mandate. The Forest Service had an opportunity to incorporate a rational, system-wide planning and managerial process that would promote multiple use in perpetuity. But it blew it. The service demonstrated, once again, how difficult it is to effect change in a bureaucracy. The voices of reason and conservation within the Forest Service itself have been squelched or driven out. The service has produced a total of 107 resource management plans, and conservationists have appealed every last one of them. The appeals process is an arduous one, requiring hard work by hundreds of dedicated conservationists all across the nation, and appeals are not undertaken lightly. Nonetheless, the management plans have been so biased and unbalanced, favoring the timber industry to the detriment of all other users, that volunteers have manned the battlements to save the nation's forests. The Forest Service has responded by attempting to make an appeal more difficult than ever.

The Land and Resource Management Plan for the National Forests in Texas seemed less inflammatory than other plans, simply because the Texas forests are less spectacular, lacking the magnificent old-growth conifers of the Pacific coast and western states. Nevertheless, it was sufficient to prod Texans into action. The Texas plan considered 13 alternatives for managing the 634,912 acres in 4 national forests. The critical issues were the amount of timber to be harvested and the manner in which it was to be cut.

The Forest Plan increased the amount of timber to be cut by 22 percent, to 126.3 million board feet annually. The harvest methods were to be clearcutting (60 percent) and seedtree cutting (40 percent). Each year 6,384 acres of forest were to be "regenerated." "Regeneration" is the euphemism used by the Forest Service to describe the conversion of a forest to an open field, devoid of trees. Loggers cut and remove all the marketable trees. The remaining trees are knocked down and piled in long windrows, allowed to dry, and eventually burned. Within 5 years of the clearcut, pine seedlings of a single species are transplanted to the cleared field. The result is a monoculture tree farm where pines, all of the same species and age, grow into an even-aged "forest." A seedtree cut amounts to little more than a slow clearcut. At harvest, 2 to 10 pine trees per acre are left standing. These trees produce seeds, which are dispersed by the wind, enabling new trees to sprout and grow up around the seedtrees. Once an adequate number of seedlings have become established, the seedtrees themselves are harvested. The final result, in 5 to 10 years, is a large field filled with pine seedlings and devoid of large trees—in other words, a two-stage clearcut.

As one can easily imagine, the result of a clearcut or seedtree cut is devastating to a red-cockaded woodpecker, an obligate forest species. An open field, where grasses and other herbaceous vegetation soon grow taller than the pine seedlings, is completely unattractive to red-cockaded woodpeckers. To a flicker, an ant-eating ground forager, yes; to a redheaded woodpecker, an open-habitat flycatcher, perhaps, if a dead snag remained to perch upon; but to an old-pine-loving forest dweller like the red-cockaded, never. It is true that you can visit red-cockaded colonies where clearcuts extend right up to the foot of the cavity trees and the birds are still present. The birds do not die of shock or trauma from witnessing the destruction of their foraging territory. They are just forced to forage elsewhere. But if "surplus" suitable foraging territory is not immediately adjacent to their colony trees, and it seldom is, the supply of resources necessary for survival declines. Remember, the woodpeckers are tied to their cavity trees, utilized for decades and inherited from their forebears.

If the woodpeckers are forced to travel farther to forage, the birds may burn more energy flying to and from the distant foraging habitat than is contained in the food they capture. If suitable foraging habitat is available only on the far side of the clearcut, it also becomes dangerous, because the woodpeckers must fly above open fields, where they are exposed to hawks. Many kinds of birds go to great lengths to follow treelines and avoid crossing open areas. The woodpecker always remains predator-conscious in the forest. It gives voice to alarm calls when it spots a hawk and immediately changes its behavior, clinging to the far side of a tree trunk, taking wing only when forced to by the predator.

People have observed red-cockadeds in seedtree cuts. But their presence there, from habit or lack of choice, does not indicate that they are doing well. Persistence of the birds depends on reproduction, which directly correlates with body condition, which is linked to adequate food resources. The production of one to four eggs is the most energy- and resource-demanding chore of any female woodpecker. All the nutrients and materials in those eggs are pulled directly from her body. If she is not in good health, with an excess of body materials, she cannot produce an egg. Once laid, the eggs must be incubated, virtually day and night. While the male and female are incubating, they cannot be foraging for food. If food is scarce, feeding bouts take longer, and incubation declines. Once hatched, the young woodpeckers have voracious appetites. Food resources must be abundant and close to the nest cavity. While the parents and their helpers ferry food to the nestlings every few minutes, having to fly greater distances reduces foraging efficiency and ultimately means that fewer, if any, fledglings emerge from the nest. It is very difficult to prove conclusively that timber harvest is directly responsible for population decline, but the direct loss of adjacent foraging habitat is certainly a prime suspect.

The timber harvest method preferred by environmentalists is uneven-aged, or selection, management. This system maintains continuous high forest cover. Trees are harvested at lengthy intervals, 5 to 10 years or more, and the number of trees selected for removal is equal in volume to the total incremental growth of all trees since the last harvest. Smaller trees, whose growth larger, overshadowing trees may have suppressed, are now "released" to achieve larger size. Small seedlings and saplings on the forest floor benefit from more sunlight streaming through new openings in the forest canopy above, created by the removal of the large, harvested trees. This harvest method most closely mimics life and death in a natural forest, where trees die from old age, disease, insects, wind, or fire, eventually decaying and falling to the ground, where decomposing organisms recycle the stored nutrients. Trees of all ages, from seedling to ancient, live side by side at all times; hence it is termed an uneven-aged forest.

Uneven-aged management can select single trees or groups of trees for harvest. It can even accommodate clearcutting if it is held to an acre or two in size. Such losses mimic natural events like insect outbreaks, hurricane or tornado windthrow, or hot fires. Natural forests typically are a mosaic of small, even-aged patches scattered across an uneven-aged matrix. Unfortunately the forest industry likes to think big when it comes to clearcutting. Its methods are analogous to search-and-destroy tactics; it searches for and harvests all the marketable trees and destroys what remains. This practice may encompass single patches as large as several hundred acres. Forest Service abuses of clearcutting became so excessive that the 1976 National Forest Management Act specified that clearcutting should be used only where it is the optimum method. Unfortunately the Forest Service regards it as the optimum method everywhere. Congress further specified that clearcut patches not exceed 80 acres in southern yellow pine forests. Naturally the Forest Service cuts as close to 80 acres as often as it can.

The principal point of contention between advocates of the two management systems is the resultant landscape. Clearcutting totally destroys the forest. It is the most blatant example on earth of the old adage that one "cannot see for the forest for the trees." Professional "foresters" view trees as dollar signs, harvest them all, and replant monoculture tree farms, which no more resemble a forest than a wheat field resembles a multispecies prairie. Foresters focus on the financial maturity of a pine tree, that point in its life beyond which the tree's slower growth makes it no longer profitable to keep it standing. This point usually occurs when the pine reaches 20 inches, or less, in diameter. Environmentalists prefer to focus on the biological or physiological maturity of a pine tree, that point in its life when resistance to adverse influences (disease, insects, etc.) is so low that death or a net loss in tree volume is likely to occur, generally reached at about 30 inches of diameter for loblolly or shortleaf pines. Foresters classify stands of old trees as "overaged," "overmature," or "decadent"; red-cockaded woodpeckers view them as prime habitat.

It is important to note that the adoption of even-aged management is a relatively new action. The Forest Service first initiated this strategy about 1950 and introduced it in the Texas national forests about 1964. Even-aged management creates 10-year age-classes, a grouping that works well for computer processing. The number of classes depends on the rotation age—that is, the maximum age that trees will be allowed to attain before harvest. If the pine trees are to be harvested in 60 years, then one-sixth of the forest will be in each age-class, as 0–10, 10–20, 20–30, 30–40, 40–50, and 50–60 years. Because even-aged management is so new, no one in the United States has ever taken a forest through a complete sawlog rotation. There has not been enough time. Thus it has not been proved that this "fast tree farming" will work, particularly past a second generation. Some academicians doubt that we can continue to extract nutrients from the soil at this rate and sustain rapid growth through several harvest cycles.

There is also a more practical aspect. In Texas the Forest Service plans to rotate loblolly pines in 70 years and shortleaf or longleaf pines in 80 years. This time frame creates a sense of urgency because the existing forest is "too old." No more than 58,000 to 66,000 acres (one-eighth or one-seventh) of the pine forest should constitute any one age-class. There are 36,000 acres of 90-year-old trees (horrors! Too old!). There are 97,000 acres of 70-year-old pines and 103,000 acres of 60-year-old trees, too many to fit in the age-class pigeonholes. To correct this imbalance, the Forest Plan will regenerate 64,000 acres in its first decade. Just as the forest is getting old enough to support red-cockaded woodpeckers adequately, it will be "necessary" to destroy 14 percent of the total forest, or 22 percent of 60- to 90-year-old forest capable of supporting the birds, to restore "balance" and facilitate bookkeeping.

The Texas Committee on Natural Resources (TCONR) and others appealed the Forest Plan for Texas. Since every Forest Plan in the nation had been appealed, and the Texas appeal might take years, TCONR requested that clearcutting be halted pending outcome of the appeal. The Forest Service predictably refused to do this, so TCONR, the Sierra Club, and the Wilderness Society, armed with the Conner report, the Forest Plan, and the southern pine beetle management plan, went to court. They charged that the Forest Service was conducting a virtually unrestrained timber management program in the national forests of Texas. They further claimed that the Forest Service's single-minded pursuit of timber management objectives had devastated the wilderness characteristics of designated wilderness areas in Texas and that the service had failed to manage properly, and had even destroyed, essential foraging and nesting habitats of the red-cockaded woodpecker. Moreover, the adoption of even-aged management practices had increased the susceptibility of the forest to insect attack, reduced native biological diversity, and harmed numerous other nontimber uses of the forests. The Sierra Club lawyers charged that the Forest Service, in doing all the above, had violated the Endangered Species Act, the Wilderness Act, the National Environmental Policy Act, and the National Forest Management Act.

These were rather sweeping charges to level at a federal agency charged with obeying and enforcing federal laws. The Forest Service denied that even-aged management adversely affected the woodpecker, native biological diversity, or the susceptibility of the forests to insect attack. The court rejected challenges to the Forest Plan and the southern pine beetle control program, which were already under appeal. While the court acknowledged that the Conner report demonstrated considerable woodpecker decline in recent years, it was not absolutely clear that even-aged management was the causal factor. The court agreed to hear further argument that a "taking" of the woodpeckers had occurred and ordered the Forest Service temporarily to refrain from cutting within 1,200 feet of a red-cockaded woodpecker colony in the national forests.

Section 9 of the Endangered Species Act prohibits the "taking" of an endangered species, with "taking" including any act or attempt to harass, harm, pursue, hunt, or wound any individual of the species. "Harass" is defined by the act as any intentional or negligent act or omission which creates the likelihood of injury to wildlife by annoying it to such an extent as to disrupt significantly normal behavior. It defines "harm" as an act which actually kills or injures wildlife, including significant habitat modification or degradation that kills or injures wildlife by significantly impairing essential behavior patterns, including breeding, feeding, or sheltering. For many years this remained a gray area. If you shot a red-cockaded woodpecker, you had obviously broken the law. But suppose you merely chopped down its cavity tree? The bird was still alive and well, but you had removed its critical shelter. Had you violated the law?

A small yellow-headed, parrot-billed finchlike bird from Hawaii helped resolve the issue and simultaneously carved out a niche for itself in law history. To protect this endangered species, the palila, the Sierra Club sued the state of Hawaii in the name of the bird *(Palila v. Hawaii Department of Natural Resources)*. The court ordered the state to remove introduced mouflon sheep from critical habitat for the bird which the sheep were destroying. The court found that "harm" requires neither the death of individual members of the species nor a finding that habitat degradation is presently driving the species farther toward extinction. Habitat destruction that prevents the *recovery* of the species by affecting essential behavior patterns causes actual injury to the species and constitutes a "taking" under Section 9 of the Endangered Species Act. This court ruling added a powerful weapon to the environmentalist arsenal.

The Endangered Species Act was further demonstrated to

have teeth in 1987. A development company planned to build 4,500 houses near Ocala, Florida, but discovered that red-cockaded woodpeckers might hinder their project. Two company officers decided to eliminate the problem by taking the matter into their own hands. They killed two woodpeckers with shotguns and had about 200 cavity trees cut down. The men were reported, were arrested, and pleaded guilty to one count of a federal indictment alleging they "took" red-cockaded woodpeckers. The president and the CEO of the construction company received two years' probation and a $300,000 fine earmarked for woodpecker recovery projects. The court ordered the company to set aside 40 acres within the development for wildlife habitat and provide another 150 acres of protected habitat adjacent to a state or national park. The total sentence amounted to about $1 million.

The Sierra Club charged that the Forest Service in Texas had violated the Endangered Species Act in two ways. First, it claimed that forest management activities had resulted in "takings" of red-cockaded woodpeckers and jeopardized their continued existence. The 125 acres of foraging habitat the Forest Service allotted to each woodpecker clan were the minimum required, not the average or maximum size, and thus were contributing to the decline of woodpecker populations. In addition, the average age of pine trees selected by the woodpeckers in Texas for new cavity trees was more than 100 years old. Since 80-year rotations would eliminate the possibility of any new trees reaching an age of 100 years, the woodpeckers would have no chance of expanding their populations. Also, cutting pines to suppress southern pine beetle outbreaks destroyed prime woodpecker nesting and foraging habitat. Finally, the Forest Service had, on numerous occasions, violated its own Wildlife Habitat Management Guidelines for the woodpecker, resulting in the destruction of cavity trees and abandonment of colonies.

Secondly, the Sierra Club charged that the Forest Service had also violated the Endangered Species Act by failing to reinitiate formal consultation with the U.S. Fish and Wildlife Service. Section 7 of the act mandates that each federal agency shall ensure that any action authorized, funded, or carried out by the agency is not likely to "jeopardize" the continued existence of an endangered species. To "jeopardize," in this context, has been defined as engaging in an action that reasonably would be expected, directly or indirectly, to reduce appreciably the likelihood of either survival *or recovery* in the wild by reducing the reproduction, numbers, or distribution of the endangered species. If any possibility of such jeopardy exists, the agency must seek a formal "consultation" with the Fish and Wildlife Service (FWS), which administers the Endangered Species Act, following which the FWS may issue a Biological Opinion.

Sierra Club attorneys reasoned that because the Conner report provided new information documenting the precipitous decline of active red-cockaded colonies and populations and because it concluded that the species was in danger of extirpation in Texas in the near future, the act required the Forest Service to initiate a formal consultation with the Fish and Wildlife Service. It seemed clear that the 1985 Recovery Plan recommendations and Forest Service management guidelines were ineffective. The Recovery Plan and management guidelines were designed to double the total number of red-cockaded colonies. Instead, the population had been halved. The Forest Service had relied heavily on the establishment of replacement and recruitment stands to preserve woodpecker nesting habitat while permitting the harvest of old trees and short timber harvest rotation cycles. The FWS Biological Opinion certifying the adequacy of the management guidelines assumed that the concept of replacement and recruitment stands was a viable strategy. The Conner report concluded that replacement and recruitment stands were ineffective. No new active colonies had arisen in the Angelina NF for 10 years. Newly established colonies had become extremely rare across the entire range of the woodpecker.

Thus the stage was set. Old hands associated with one or both recovery plans, and with years of mutually respected research, gathered in the courtroom in Tyler, Texas, that March day in 1988, but the camaraderie was missing. The government biologists were ill at ease, being asked as they were to provide technical guidelines and testimony in support of a policy some might privately disavow. Greetings were perfunctory and correctly polite.

This drama revealed the ultimate tragedy of the legal system: It forces one to choose sides. The biologists, if left alone, could readily agree on a woodpecker management strategy. Certainly there would be differences of opinion. If you gather a half dozen experts on anything, you are likely to get seven opinions, for at least one of them will be unable to make up his or her mind. But the differences could be readily resolved because the margin of error should favor the woodpecker; after all, extinction is forever. Unfortunately forest managers, typically unconcerned about the woodpecker to begin with and frustrated by challenges to their management skills and competency, will not permit the biologists to select management policy that will ensure woodpecker survival. So a confrontation was established, pitting one set of experts against the other.

Judge Robert Parker quickly established the ground rules. The Conner report and the videotaped testimony of Jerome Jackson, former recovery team leader, at that moment seeking ivory-billed woodpeckers in Cuba, would form the bulwark of the testimony. No testimony regarding the national forest management plan or the southern pine beetle environmental impact statement would be permitted unless it was directly related to the red-cockaded woodpecker. The opposing attorneys were instructed to select their best witness to make each point and forgo repetition.

A parade of witnesses addressed the biology and ecological requirements of red-cockaded woodpeckers, habitat characteristics, forest fragmentation, habitat islands and extinction, forest management practices, timber harvesting techniques, and what constitutes a forest. Judge Parker elicited recommendations from the witnesses on what needed to be done to save the woodpecker. In four days it was over.

In June 1988 the court handed down its opinion. The Forest Service was stunned. Judge Parker stated that "the voluminous evidence . . . leaves this Court with the firm persuasion that we are presiding over the last rites of this cohabitant of the blue planet." The court found that the woodpecker population had declined 76 percent on the Sabine National Forest (1978–87), 41 percent on the Davy Crockett NF (1983–87), and 42 percent on the Angelina NF (1983–87) and that the entire population in Texas national forests would be extinct by 1995 if no changes were made in forest management practices.

The causes of this rapid decline were found to be: (1) fragmentation of habitat by clearcutting practices which resulted in separation of nesting and foraging areas; (2) clearcutting within foraging areas which reduced foraging habitat available to birds within their effective range; (3) clearcutting within 200 feet of actual colony sites and, in some instances, even up to cavity trees; (4) failure to control hardwood midstory encroachment around cavity trees in colony sites, around potential cavity trees in sites adjacent to colonies, and in foraging areas; (5) failure to employ regular prescribed fire in colony and foraging areas to control hardwood and young pine encroachment; (6) failure to provide an appropriate basal area in colony and potential recruitment stand sites; (7) lack of available cavity trees of sufficient age—100 plus years—as the result of silvicultural practices employed over the past 20 years by the Forest Service; (8) disruption of colony areas from the establishment of logging roads and the utilization of regularly traveled off-pavement roadways through site areas; (9) damage to colony site and foraging area habitat trees by logging trucks and logging equipment; and (10) failure to identify and preserve mature trees containing red heart in habitat areas.

The court further found that for the past 8 years the Forest Service budget had provided only 10 percent of the funds necessary to manage the woodpecker according to guidelines set forth in the Forest Service wildlife management handbook and had provided no funds for mid-story removal. Funds received from the sale of timber on clearcut tracts were available as discretionary funds for use in woodpecker management, but no such funds had been committed to red-cockaded woodpecker habitat preservation. The Forest Service had never fully implemented the red-cockaded woodpecker management handbook plans, prepared in 1973, for habitat preservation or improvement or for control of the hardwood mid-story in the Texas national forests. Controlling the hardwood mid-story is essential to the maintenance of the woodpecker colonies. The court found that clearcut areas are not suitable for foraging by the woodpeckers for at least 30 years from the date of reforestation, resulting in fragmentation of the forest, isolation of colonies, and shunning of clearcut areas for 30 years by the woodpeckers. Old trees—100 years or more—containing red heart are essential for bird survival and for establishing new or replacement colony trees. Any program that provides for harvesting these old trees mitigates against survival of the species in the Texas national forests. Sixty-square-foot basal area is the optimum density, taking into consideration the requirements of the woodpecker and factors relating to control of the southern pine beetle. Any rotation period of cutting by even-aged management methods (clearcutting) that is economically advantageous to the Forest Service is incompatible with the survival of the woodpecker within colony and foraging habitat areas.

The court also analyzed clearcutting versus selection management and was persuaded of the following facts: (1) Selection management has an initial 20 to 25 percent economic advantage over clearcutting because of the necessity of artificially seeding clearcut tracts; (2) uneven-aged or selection management produces more wood per dollar spent and is economically more efficient over the productive life of a tract of timber; (3) uniformity is best served by even-aged management; (4) even-aged stands are more susceptible to southern pine beetle infestation; (5) economic factors mitigate in favor of selection management; and (6) the sole reason for the Forest Service's adoption of even-aged or clearcutting as the management method of choice is the fact that it is preferred by the timber companies. The Forest Service had experienced a high degree of the "revolving door" phenomenon between government and private interests, providing an incentive for agency personnel to accommodate industry desires, which explained the high level of influence the timber companies have over policies and practices of the Forest Service.

The court characterized the Conner report as the best evaluation and study of the crisis facing the bird and of the management practices which are essential to its survival. Judge Parker designated a number of practices recommended by the report to be adopted and implemented without delay if extirpation was to be avoided.

The court concluded that the Forest Service's actions constituted a "taking" of red-cockaded woodpeckers under Section 9 of the Endangered Species Act and that past Forest Service management techniques and practices had violated Section 7 of the act. The court stated that "endangered species, unlike timber, are not renewable resources." Citing the act's provision that the various federal agencies must "insure that any action authorized, funded, or carried out by such agency . . . is not likely to jeopardize the continued existence of any endangered species or threatened species," Judge Parker noted that the Supreme Court had commented that "one would be hard pressed to find a statutory provision whose terms were any plainer" and that "Congress intended to halt and reverse the trend towards species extinction, whatever the cost."

Judge Parker cited all four factors in the regulations defining "harm"—significant impairment of essential behavioral patterns, including breeding, feeding, or sheltering. First, the woodpecker colonies had been isolated from one another in "islands" of older-growth stands surrounded by clearcuts, impairing essential woodpecker behavior patterns. Second, colony isolation interfered with breeding practices because dispersing young females would have difficulty finding males, resulting in a reduced gene pool. Third, clearcutting close to colonies limited the available foraging areas, and harvesting older pines reduced foraging quality. Finally, even-aged management had eliminated the older stands of pines needed for cavity construction. These actions "jeopardized" the species within the meaning of the act.

The court concluded that the Forest Service had failed to take the steps necessary to ensure that its management practices would not jeopardize the woodpeckers. Furthermore, the Conner report offered relevant new information that pointed out the deficiencies in current forest management practices, requiring reinitiation of formal consultation with the U.S. Fish and Wildlife Service. In Judge Parker's view, "what this case really boils down to is the Forest Service's implementation of practices identified by its own experts and recognized by its own documents as critical to save this bird from extinction."

The court granted a permanent injunction against even-aged forest management within 1,200 meters of identified active and inactive red-cockaded woodpecker colony sites in the national forests of Texas. It ordered the Forest Service to (1) convert forest harvesting techniques within 1,200 meters of any colony site to a program of selection or uneven-aged management that preserved "old-growth" pines from cutting; (2) establish a pine basal area of 60 square feet per acre within

1,200 meters of any colony site; (3) establish a program of mid-story removal of hardwoods in and adjacent to colony sites; and (4) discontinue the use of existing logging roads or other nonpaved roads within colony sites and restrict the use of such roadways to the essential minimum within 1,200 meters of any colony site. The Forest Service was granted 60 days to produce a Comprehensive Plan designed to meet the court specifications and maximize the probability of survival of the woodpeckers in Texas national forests. Judge Parker directed that the Comprehensive Plan not be restricted to techniques described in the Forest Service handbook or the Recovery Plan and that it should provide a monitoring mechanism for the plan itself and for periodic review and evaluation of the techniques to be employed.

Environmentalists rejoiced that the woodpecker, like the palila, had won its day in court. Sierra Club attorney Douglas Honnold, who had successfully argued the woodpeckers' case before Judge Parker, was quick to point out the national significance of this victory in Texas. Several legal firsts had been established. This was the first case in which a court had found that a Section 9 taking of an endangered species occurred despite the absence of a designated critical habitat for the species. It was also the first case in which a court found a violation of the Endangered Species Act despite the fact that the defendant agency had complied with the provisions of the Recovery Plan for the species. While the Recovery Plan required only 125 acres of foraging habitat per colony, the 1,200-meter zone would provide 1,118 acres. This was also the first case in which a court found that the agencies' actions were likely to "jeopardize" the continued existence of the species despite the fact that the Fish and Wildlife Service has issued a "no jeopardy" decision concerning the activities. Previous no jeopardy decisions had discouraged environmentalists from challenging agency actions that appeared to harm other endangered species.

From a forestry standpoint, this court decision was the

most significant prohibition against clearcutting since the 1976 National Forest Management Act had limited the size of clearcuts. The 1,200-meter criterion (3,936 feet, or three-quarters of a mile) would encircle 1,118 acres surrounding each woodpecker colony and might permanently stop clear-cutting on one-third, or 200,000 acres, of the Texas national forests. Some overlap would occur as the circles were plotted, but the Forest Service itself would also experience forest frag-mentation firsthand, as the circles isolated small parcels of forest too small to manage independently. The service re-mained free to practice even-aged management outside the woodpecker zones. It is also important to note that tree har-vest has not been prohibited within the woodpecker zones. Trees can still be cut individually or in small groups, but large parcels cannot be clearcut, as the forest industry prefers. As Honnold prophetically stated, "we have reason to celebrate, and can expect industry backlash."

In July 1988 the Forest Service suspended five logging oper-ations that were in progress and eighteen operations for which bids had been accepted, all because they were within the 1,200-meter zone. In addition, 473 miles of roads, mostly unimproved dead-end logging roads, were closed. In August logging trucks emerged from the east Texas pineywoods and homed in on Forest Service headquarters in Lufkin like a swarm of pine beetles, circling the Federal Building to protest the court order limiting timber harvesting. One truck towed a sign urging spectators: SEND WOODPECKER PIES TO [TCONR leader Ned] FRITZ, THE JUDGE, AND GOODTIME CHARLIE [Con-gressman Charles Wilson]. U.S. Senator Phil Gramm was en-listed to meet with Forest Service Chief Dale Robertson and urge him to appeal the court ruling. A plethora of misinfor-mation, some of it emanating from current or retired Forest Service employees, surfaced in the news media. The Angelina County Farm Bureau attacked the notion that the red-cock-aded woodpecker was endangered and the credibility of the

Conner report and claimed that the court ruling would be ecologically harmful to the forest. While logging interests claimed that logging jobs would be lost, some older foresters, who recalled the days when uneven-aged management was the preferred method of the Forest Service, predicted that the return to selective cutting and smaller equipment would increase logging jobs while preserving the forest.

In August 1988 the Forest Service submitted an incredulous Comprehensive Plan for the management of red-cockaded woodpecker habitat and a plea for the court to reverse its decision. A task force comprised of three foresters and one wildlife biologist had consulted with a number of specialists within the Forest Service and produced a distorted interpretation of the court order that could justify "business as usual" forest management.

The plan purported to provide, as directed by the court, priority treatment of active (but not inactive) colonies, treatment of entire colony sites, aggressive prescribed burning and control of hardwood mid-story, preservation of relict old-growth trees, provision of additional foraging habitat, closure of primitive roads in colonies, and prohibition of new road construction in colonies. But the plan focused on the court's mandate to "maximize the probability of survival of the red-cockaded woodpeckers in the national forests of Texas" and claimed that several court-ordered actions were inconsistent with this mandate. The Forest Service specifically objected to the order to convert to selection or uneven-aged management harvesting techniques, use of aggressive prescribed burning with uneven-aged management, and a reduction of pine stocking to 60 square feet of basal area. In exchange for excision of the heart of the court plan, the Forest Service proposed to substitute, within the 1,200-meter zone, a 120-year rotation with even-aged management, regeneration by a "modified shelterwood" approach, no regeneration within 400 meters (one-fourth mile) of active colony sites for at least ten years, thinning to a basal area of 60 to 100 square feet, and control of hardwood mid-story within colony sites, recruitment, and replacement stands.

In its 1985 draft Land and Resource Management Plan for the national forests in Texas the Forest Service had proposed harvesting pine trees at 40 to 90 years of age, with 51 percent of the timber harvested on a 50-year rotation. When the final plan was issued in 1987, rotation ages had been changed to 70 and 80 years. The 1979 red-cockaded woodpecker Recovery Plan had recommended 80 years for loblolly and shortleaf pines and 100 years for longleaf pine trees. The 1985 Recovery Plan failed to recommend a rotation age. The AOU committee had recommended rotations greater than 80 years of age and large tracts of old growth. These recommendations were ignored by the Forest Service. Now that the court had ordered uneven-aged management in red-cockaded woodpecker habitat, the service offered to extend rotations to 120 years which amounted to "too little, too late."

The Forest Service emphasized that the 120-year rotation regimen would provide one-sixth of the total acreage in 100-plus-year-old stands, and 75 percent of the total acreage would be greater than 30 years old, providing suitable forage trees. Of course, this meant that 25 percent of the forest would be unsuitable for woodpecker foraging at all times, and these stands would continue to fragment the forest. Uneven-aged management would retain 100-plus-year-old trees in all stands, providing potential cavity trees throughout the forest, and suitable foraging trees of 30 plus years in 100 percent of the forest, while totally eliminating forest fragmentation.

Since the Forest Service thought that a disproportionate amount of the existing forest stands were 50 to 90 years old, its stated goal was to "redistribute" this "imbalance" and create younger stands so that no more than one-third of the forest would be of this age. Yet these older forest stands constituted the very habitat in which the woodpecker persisted and represented the sole hope for expansion of the population into presently unoccupied forest. It is difficult to understand how a reduction in the amount of acreage which can potentially develop into old-growth forest could possibly benefit the woodpeckers. Although no existing forest stands were 120 years old, there would be no moratorium on harvesting. The Forest Service offered to carry existing 70-plus-year-old stands to rotation age "unless not permitted by site and stand conditions, or unless necessary to improve the distribution of the age classes." With this loophole, the forest prescriptionist could harvest a stand whenever he chose.

The Forest Service questioned whether it would be possible to carry a monocultural pine stand to 120 years of age. Individual pine trees can surpass 300 years of age, but large stands of old trees are susceptible to disease and insect outbreaks. This is a valid point, and easily remedied by uneven-aged management, which would scatter the old, relict trees throughout the forest, where they are less vulnerable to pine beetles and other natural enemies.

A critical facet of even-aged management is the method of regeneration of the forest following harvest. A modified shelterwood scheme was proposed which would cut trees to a level only one-third to two-thirds that of the basal area mandated by the court. These seedtrees would be left for 2 to 15 years to permit a natural restocking of new pine seedlings on the forest floor. Then most of the seedtrees would be cut, leaving only 5 or 6 trees per acre standing. This level of tree density does not constitute a forest. The distance between trees may be five times greater than the width of the tree crowns. The resultant landscape would resemble a pine savanna, a grassland, or shrubland interspersed with trees. The woodpeckers would lose the protection of the forest canopy, which would disappear altogether. Once the bulk of the seedtrees was removed, the landscape would be essentially useless to woodpeckers for 20 to 30 years.

Furthermore, trees which grew up under crowded, competitive conditions, with a restricted root structure, would now be exposed to higher wind forces and increased probability of lightning strikes. Cavity trees in Texas and Oklahoma suffer 7 percent annual mortality. If you start with 100 trees, in 5 years only 70 remain; in 10 years only 48; less than half; in 50 years, only 3. By the time the newly regenerated pines were old enough to become cavity trees, only 1 of the original potential cavity trees would be expected to remain standing. Even this calculation does not account for increased mortality from windthrow or lightning, but it does demonstrate the cata-strophic impact of even-aged management, which casts all aspects of the forest into an all-or-nothing mold. The provi-sion of 5 or 6 large trees per regenerated acre is totally inade-quate but symbolic of the depauperate intellectual foundation of even-aged management.

The Forest Service proposed to delay all regeneration within 400 meters (1,312 feet or ¼ mile) of any active colony for a period of 10 years. This would prevent further fragmen-tation of 124 acres of foraging habitat, if we assume that all of the zone was suitable for foraging. Regeneration would there-after be permitted, unless the woodpeckers had established a new colony; in essence this amounts to a "use it or lose it" strategy.

The court had ordered that the forest be thinned to 60 square feet of basal area, to provide the open, parklike land-scape preferred by the woodpeckers. The Forest Service pro-posed thinning to 60 to 100 square feet, to provide more foraging trees for the woodpecker. Since the existing forest had 74 to 100 square feet of basal area, no thinning would be necessary, for the Forest Service did not recognize that the woodpeckers could have too many trees (an overly dense for-est) as well as too few. The Forest Service also proffered spe-cious arguments that an uneven-aged forest would be unable to regenerate itself or be unable to withstand frequent burn-ing, positions readily countered by its own publications.

The service argued that uneven-aged management would result in a fragile and unpredictable regeneration system that would jeopardize the long-term provision of red-cockaded woodpecker habitat. Its timber-oriented managers apparently failed to recognize that the critical status of the bird demanded immediate and drastic short-term changes in forest management. Although nature had regenerated uneven-aged forests for thousands of years, forests in which the woodpecker had evolved and thriven, the Forest Service, in essence, believed it could not duplicate this pattern. Instead, it tried to convince Judge Parker that the management scheme he ordered would lead to the extinction of the bird. The Forest Service argued that minor modifications to the even-aged management style it preferred, but never found in nature, would be the bird's salvation. The very management which was the prime suspect for placing the species in jeopardy would miraculously save the day. The words of Texas Parks and Wildlife Department biologist Dan Lay, written in 1973 after studying the species in Texas for four years, were never more prescient:

> Most of the known red-cockaded woodpeckers in Texas are in uneven age stands developed with selective silviculture. The National Forests adopted even-age silviculture system in 1964, which has not yet affected the stands in which the birds occur. Most birds are present due to uneven stands. They use a scattered stand of old trees among a majority of younger trees. The reasons over-age trees are present vary. Some have red-heart disease and are unmerchantable. Some are in such young stands and in such low numbers that there is not enough operable volume to make a sawlog sale. Some are located in stands that have not been "improved" with a sanitation cut to remove high risk trees. Such relict over-age trees will not occur in future forests with even-age treatment and 70 or 80 year rotations, as planned for the Texas national forests.

Judge Parker wisely rejected the Forest Service management plan, demonstrating that wearing a black judicial gown does not predispose one to being hoodwinked. He ordered submission of another plan which followed his court order. The Forest Service did so and appealed his decision.

The Sierra Club next moved to expand the protection which Judge Parker had provided for Texas woodpeckers to other parts of the South. In December 1988 it filed the obligatory 60-day notice of intent-to-sue letters to national forest managers in Alabama, Arkansas, Florida, Georgia, Kentucky, Louisiana, Mississippi, and North Carolina. The Forest Service reluctantly agreed to negotiate a settlement, and teams of lawyers and biologists representing both sides once again converged on Texas. The March 1989 settlement addressed forest management during a 2-year interim period while the Forest Service rewrote its management guidelines. The Forest Service agreed to forgo all clearcutting within 1,200 meters of any active or inactive woodpecker colony. It would utilize a modified shelterwood harvest method which would not remove the sheltering trees during the interim period.

The honeymoon was short-lived. The Sierra Club attorneys, in filing their briefs addressing the appeal of Judge Parker's decision by the Forest Service attorneys, noted an inconsistency in the Forest Service position. On the one hand, the service was arguing before the court of appeals that Judge Parker had erred in reaching his decision and formulating his court order. On the other hand, it had essentially agreed to extend a close approximation of Judge Parker's management plan to national forests in other states. Apparently the timber beasts within the Forest Service won the day, for by June 1989 the service had reneged on the settlement agreement. One step forward and two steps back. Dancers, find your partners and return to court.

Meanwhile, another intense struggle was occurring. Section 7 of the Endangered Species Act required that the Forest Service Comprehensive Management Plan for the red-cockaded woodpecker on national forest lands in Texas be submitted to the Fish and Wildlife Service for review. In turn, the

Fish and Wildlife Service was required to issue a Biological Opinion stating that the proposed management plan would or would not jeopardize the woodpecker populations. The Forest Service strategy was simple. If the Fish and Wildlife Service could be forced to issue an opinion stating that Judge Parker's plan would cause the woodpecker to become extinct, the Forest Service would have a strong case to ask the Fifth Circuit Court of Appeals to overrule Judge Parker.

In February 1989 the Fish and Wildlife Service assembled an advisory team of woodpecker specialists that included biologists who had testified on both sides of the issue before Judge Parker. In the absence of legal trappings the atmosphere was far more congenial. The main issue remained even-aged versus uneven-aged forest management. Would uneven-aged management lead to a "shortage" of old pine trees in five or more decades? Proponents of uneven-aged management were outnumbered, but a consensus position quickly developed. Patch size was the answer. Avoidance of emotion-laden terminology and modification of standard practice were the key.

Small patches of forest would be harvested, ranging from 5 to 15 acres in size, but the average must be 10 acres or less. Such small patches might inconvenience the woodpeckers, but they would not fragment the habitat. The harvest technique would be a modified shelterwood cut. Timber cutters would leave more trees standing (40 square feet of basal area) to reseed the forest, which they would not remove in a second cut after reseeding was accomplished; thus it would not be a clearcut. Thinning of the pine trees, to control southern pine beetle outbreaks, and of the hardwood trees, to improve the habitat for woodpeckers, would extend to the entire 1,200-meter zone around each active and abandoned woodpecker colony. Thinning and hardwood control were limited to the colony site and the replacement and recruitment stands in the Comprehensive Management Plan. Thus this compromise could be viewed as true give-and-take rather than as a chipping away at core issues. Neither side would be pleased, but the bird actually may have gained a step.

At this point wildlife biologists and politicians collided once again. To complicate the issue, two different regions of the Fish and Wildlife Service were involved. The Albuquerque region drafted the opinion because it was a Texas issue, but the Atlanta region wanted more influence because geographically it regulated more habitat for the species. The power struggle rocked back and forth between the regions and between the Fish and Wildlife Service and the Forest Service.

In September 1989 the Jeopardy Biological Opinion was issued. The Fish and Wildlife Service ruled that the Comprehensive Management Plan for Texas would require implementation of an unproved system of forest management, would require an unattainable level of forest administration and intensive management, would prevent a sustained yield of suitable habitat for the woodpecker, and would preclude woodpecker populations from increasing to a size sufficient for long-term viability.

The Biological Opinion offered a "reasonable and prudent alternative" that would avoid jeopardizing the bird. Shelterwood harvest could be employed, cutting down to 30 square feet of basal area on patches averaging 25 acres in size. Sheltering trees would be retained a minimum of 5 years and then reduced to 5 or 6 trees per acre, restoring 120-year clearcut rotations as a management option. Once again the Forest Service had won the federal power struggle. Once again the red-cockaded woodpecker had lost. Fifteen days later Hurricane Hugo hurled its fury against the South Carolina coast and leveled the Francis Marion National Forest, cutting a swath 50 miles wide and 100 miles long. Treetops snapped off and were blown away, leaving a matchstick forest in their stead. Snug woodpecker cavities suddenly became roofless, as the cavity became the "weak link" in the tree trunk. In a few

short but terrifying hours 90 percent of the world's best patch
of habitat for red-cockaded woodpeckers was ruined for
decades to come, and one-fourth of the world's red-cockaded
woodpeckers were threatened with instant death or slow starvation.

POSTSCRIPT: In March 1991 the Fifth Circuit Court of Appeals affirmed Judge Parker's rulings that the Forest Service
had violated both Section 9 and Section 7 of the Endangered
Species Act in that the service's management practices had
resulted in a taking of an endangered species and were likely
to "jeopardize" the continued existence of the red-cockaded
woodpecker. The court of appeals specified that the district
court could either approve or disapprove the Forest Service
timber management plan, but it should not mandate in advance the specific features that an approvable plan should
contain.

Epilogue

SPECIES GO EXTINCT one individual at a time. For decades the red-cockaded woodpecker has been losing its grip on existence. A stillness has descended on the pine forests as the chatter of this little bird has ceased to be heard. Colony after colony has winked out forever, leaving empty cavity trees standing as mute sentinels marking their passage. Legislative acts and lawsuits have failed to stem the tide. The bird has lacked an effective advocate.

On private lands the species has suffered from the tyranny of numerous small decisions or no decisions at all. The bird is truly a victim of benign neglect. Barely noticed except for its resin-drenched cavity trees, its contributions to forest ecology

245

go unheralded. Even landowners uninterested in forest product harvest have unwittingly contributed to the bird's demise
as hardwood trees slowly rise, in the absence of fire, to dominate the forest and change its physical aspect. The landscape
grinds inexorably toward a climax hardwood forest. The
woodpecker is a mid-successional forest species which has lost
its most valuable ally: wildfire. The bird will not make its last
stand on earth on private property. That battle has already
been lost, and there is little prospect for change. The small
landowners, even those of a mind to save the bird, do not
control sufficient habitat. The corporate owners of large land-
holdings may be willing to spare and maintain colony sites,
but long-rotation management of extensive foraging areas for
the birds is unlikely to be adopted.

The future of the red-cockaded woodpecker rests with
beneficial management of public lands: the national forests,
wildlife refuges, and military reservations. This fact has long
been recognized by everyone except key decision makers in
the controlling agencies. Change is the critical issue. How can
one get bloated bureaucracies to change their ways?

The problem is not a lack of information. Woodpecker
biologists have known for decades what action is needed to
save the bird. Ignorance can be overcome, but apparently we
cannot cure stupidity. The problem is not a lack of legal authority. The Endangered Species Act has the teeth to save
this bird, but no one cares to use them for an effective bite. It
is a curious anomaly that in the world of macho hunters and
fishermen the Fish and Wildlife Service has come to be dominated by males without testicular hormones. A nagging suspi-
cion lingers that all it will take is one successful prosecution of
a real, live bureaucrat for failing to protect the endangered
red-cockaded woodpecker. One threat of a prison sentence
may change a lot of attitudes across the piedmont, the coastal
plain, and along the banks of the Potomac.

The working biologists of the Fish and Wildlife Service,
genuinely concerned about the bird, know what needs to be

done and have repeatedly submitted their management recommendations. Inevitably these pleas are watered down at
the regional level and disappear upon crossing the Potomac
River to the land of the "go along to get along" mentality.
Even if the Fish and Wildlife Service were struck with an urge
to force the Forest Service to obey the law, both agencies are
represented by the U.S. attorney general, perhaps the most
conspicuous conflict of interest within our government. This
obstacle seems insurmountable.

Ironically the Forest Service knows about the woodpecker
as much as, perhaps more than, anyone. Its biologists have
argued forcibly within the service and published their findings and recommendations both within and outside the service, but to little, if any, avail. Entrenched attitudes and a
narrow focus on timber and fiber production blind too many
people to the discrepancies between Forest Service legislative
mandates and management actions. The research arm of the
service is one of the largest natural resource organizations in
the world, yet researchers despair that so little of their output
seems to be incorporated into national forest management,
particularly regarding the red-cockaded woodpecker. Yet the
Forest Service remains the sole hope for preservation of the
bird.

We have learned some management tricks which appear to
help the bird. Enlarged cavities have been rehabilitated by
sheet metal "excluders" pierced by small holes or slotted entrances. The woodpeckers readily pass through the entrances,
but larger birds or other animals are blocked out and cannot
enlarge the holes. New cavities have been partially constructed by portable electric generators and power drills. The
woodpeckers readily accept these rough cavities and quickly
apply the finishing touches necessary to make them livable. It
may be possible to create a "colony" of cavity trees in suitable
habitat unoccupied by woodpeckers and introduce surplus
birds during years of good production elsewhere. Immature
females have been successfully transplanted into the territo-

ries of single males, establishing a breeding pair. Even old-growth forest can be simulated by selective harvest to preserve the oldest available trees.

Are these woodpeckers really disappearing? Many people in the Forest Service and the wood products industry have claimed for years that the species is not really endangered at all. Much of the Forest Service effort has been aimed at specifying when the species can be delisted and proclaimed "recovered." Consider the following. The birds that Dave Ligon studied are extinct. The birds that Wilson Baker studied are extinct. Most of the birds that Dan Lay studied are gone. The birds that Joe Skorupa and I studied declined to just three males before transplantation experiments began. Most of the birds that Jerry Jackson studied, in several different states, are nearly gone. Are we detecting a trend?

We clearly are running out of time. Several national forests have already lost their woodpeckers: the Uwharrie, Sumter, Caney, and Tombigbee. Three others have a single colony each: the Bankhead, Tuskegee, and Cherokee. A number of other national forests are likely to lose all their birds within a decade. We cannot complacently wait for critical decision makers to die off or retire because it is simple biological fact that human managers will easily outlive most of the birds. Two-thirds of the forests appear to have declining populations. Even the larger populations that appeared to be stable—Apalachicola National Forest and part of the Kisatchie National Forest—have one-fourth to one-third of their colonies abandoned and worrisome numbers of single-male colonies, as well as disjunct subpopulations within each forest.

Ironically the only national forest which showed any evidence of population increase was the Francis Marion National Forest in South Carolina, site of the longest intensive research program. This was the healthy showcase population, with 97 percent of the colonies active. Researchers there barely knew what an abandoned colony looked like. With an estimated 483 active colonies harboring about 1,000 woodpeckers, the population was reputed to have actually increased 10 percent over 7 years. Hurricane Hugo appears to have destroyed 50 percent of the colonies instantly and placed the remainder in serious jeopardy by ruining the timber resource which supported them. Any vestige of complacency must now be discarded. Activists have struggled to save a few birds here or an isolated colony there. A vagary of nature demonstrated that no population may be considered safe, and no population should be considered expendable. Multiple populations are essential to the long-term persistence of the species.

The red-cockaded woodpecker has survived raging forest fires and rapacious timbering at the turn of the century. It has evolved a symbiotic relationship with red heart fungus and an effective defense against arboreal snakes. It has survived episodic losses of its cavity trees and timber resources to southern pine beetles. Can it survive stewardship with the Fish and Wildlife Service and Forest Service?

Immediate action is needed to designate portions of a number of national forests for the primary purpose of increasing woodpecker populations. The harvest of forest products need not stop; indeed, it is essential that it continue. We must replace clearcutting practices with uneven-aged management or greatly modified shelterwood harvest. To save this forest woodpecker, we must first save the forest from the foresters. The implications of a perpetual thinning of the forests, as the primary harvest method, must be objectively studied by silviculturists. We must abandon as intellectually bankrupt the current "man knows better than Mother Nature" mentality. We must learn to plan and work with nature, not against it, for nature always wins. Time is on its side.

The preceding chapters have presented a number of questions and, I hope, some reasonable answers. Two questions remain. Can this woodpecker be saved from extinction? Yes, it can. We know enough about the bird to achieve that goal. We know how to manage a forest to facilitate its recovery. As yet we lack the collective will to do so. Its ultimate fate depends on the answer to a second question. How can society get the U.S. Forest Service to change its management strategy in order to preserve this woodpecker? The answer to this question must come from the realm of social science and political science, not from biological science.

The legislative branch of our government has done its part in passing the Endangered Species Act and the National Forest Management Act. The judicial branch has done its part in affirming the legality of these acts and enforcing them. It is the executive branch of government which has failed to act. If this woodpecker goes extinct, it will be due to failure of public agencies (the Department of Agriculture, Department of the Interior, and Department of Defense) to manage adequately public lands (national forests, national wildlife refuges, and military reservations). If this woodpecker is saved, it will be due to future, concerted cooperation of public-spirited citizens, environmentalists, elected officials, and appointed bureaucrats. It will be necessary to generate a public outcry, indeed an uproar, echoing coast to coast, to prevent a stillness from descending on the pines. The sound of extinction is silence—forever.

Further Readings

The two most "concentrated" sources of information on the red-cockaded woodpecker are the two symposia volumes:

Thompson, R. L. (ed.). 1971. The ecology and management of the red-cockaded woodpecker. U.S. Dept. Interior, Bur. Sport Fisheries and Wildlife, and Tall Timbers Research Station. 188 pp.

Wood, D. A. (ed.). 1983. Red-cockaded woodpecker symposium II proceedings. State of Florida Game and Fresh Water Fish Commission. 112 pp.

Specific references, in order of appearance, are listed below.

251

CHAPTER ONE: The Third Dimension

Bailey, R. G. (comp.). 1980. Description of the ecoregions of the United States. U.S. Dept. Agriculture, Forest Service Misc. Publ. No. 1391, 77 pp.

CHAPTER TWO: What Is a Woodpecker?

Bock, W. J., and W. D. Miller. 1959. The scansorial foot of the woodpeckers, with comments on the evolution of perching and climbing feet in birds. Amer. Mus. Novitates No. 1931, 45 pp.

Burt, W. H. 1930. Adaptive modification in woodpeckers. Univ. California Publ. Zoology 32(8):455–524.

Norberg, R. A. 1981. Why foraging birds in trees should climb and hop upwards rather than downwards. Ibis 123:281–288.

CHAPTER THREE: Extinction Is Forever

Takekawa, J. Y., and E. O. Garton. 1984. How much is an evening grosbeak worth? J. Forestry 82(7):426–428.

CHAPTER FOUR: There Is No Place like This Home

Conner, R. N., and B. A. Locke. 1982. Fungi and red-cockaded woodpecker cavity trees. Wilson Bull. 94:64–70.

Jackson, J. A. 1977. Red-cockaded woodpeckers and pine red heart disease. Auk 94(1):160–163.

———. 1974. Gray rat snakes versus red-cockaded woodpeckers: predator-prey adaptations. Auk 91(2):342–347.

Rudolph, D. C., H. Kyle, and R. N. Conner. 1990. Red-cockaded woodpeckers vs. rat snakes: the effectiveness of the resin barrier. Wilson Bulletin 102(1):14–22.

Dennis, J. V. 1971. Species using red-cockaded woodpecker holes in northeastern South Carolina. Bird-Banding 42(2):79–87.

Hopkins, M. L., and T. E. Lynn. 1971. Some characteristics of red-cockaded woodpecker cavity trees and management implications in South Carolina. Pp. 72–77 *in* The ecology and management of the red-cockaded woodpecker (R. L. Thompson, ed.).

Jones, H. K., and F. T. Ott. 1973. Some characteristics of red-cockaded woodpecker cavity trees in Georgia. Oriole 38(4):33–39.

Baker, W. W. 1971. Progress report on life history studies of the red-cockaded woodpecker at Tall Timbers Research Station. Pp. 44–59 in The ecology and management of the red-cockaded woodpecker (R. L. Thompson, ed.).

Locke, B. A., and R. N. Conner. 1983. A statistical analysis of the orientation of entrances to red-cockaded woodpecker cavities. Pp. 108–109 in Red-cockaded woodpecker symposium II proceedings (D. A. Wood, ed.).

Wood, D. A. 1983. Foraging and colony habitat characteristics of the red-cockaded woodpecker in Oklahoma. Pp. 51–58 in Red-cockaded woodpecker symposium II proceedings (D. A. Wood, ed.).

Inouye, D. W. 1976. Nonrandom orientation of entrance holes to woodpecker nests in aspen trees. Condor 78:101–102.

Inouye, R. S., N. J. Huntly, and D. W. Inouye. 1981. Non-random orientation of Gila woodpecker nest entrances in saguaro cacti. Condor 83:88–89.

Crockett, A. B., and H. H. Hadow. 1975. Nest site selection by Williamson and red-naped sapsuckers. Condor 77(3):365–368.

Conner, R. N. 1975. Orientation of entrances to woodpecker nest cavities. Auk 92:371–374.

Reller, A. W. 1972. Aspects of behavioral ecology of red-headed and red-bellied woodpeckers. Amer. Midl. Natur. 88(2):270–290.

Grubb, T. C., Jr., 1982. Downy woodpecker sexes select different cavity sites; an experiment using artificial snags. Wilson Bull. 94:-577–579.

Peterson, A. W., and T. C. Grubb, Jr. 1983. Artificial trees as a cavity substrate for woodpeckers. J. Wildl. Mgmt. 47:790–798.

Short, L. L. 1979. Burdens of the Picid hole-excavating habit. Wilson Bull. 91:16–28.

CHAPTER FIVE: The Generalist, the Specialist, and
the Ecological Niche

Beal, F. E. L. 1911. Food of the woodpeckers of the United States. U.S. Dept. Agriculture Biological Survey Bull. No. 37, 64p.

Chapter Six: A Cooperative Nature

Ligon, J. D. 1970. Behavior and breeding biology of the red-cockaded woodpecker. Auk 87(2):255–278.

Lay, D. W., and D. N. Russell. 1970. Notes on the red-cockaded woodpecker in Texas. Auk 87(4):781–786.

Walters, J. R.; P. D. Doerr; and J. H. Carter III. 1988. The cooperative breeding system of the red-cockaded woodpecker. Ethology 78:275–305.

Chapter Seven: Territories Large and Small

Skorupa, J. P., and R. W. McFarlane. 1976. Seasonal variation in foraging territory of red-cockaded woodpeckers. Wilson Bull. 88:-662–665.

Hooper, R. G.; L. J. Niles; R. F. Harlow; and G. W. Wood. 1982. Home ranges of red-cockaded woodpeckers in coastal South Carolina. Auk 99:675–682.

Lawrence, L. de K. 1967. A comparative life-history study of four species of woodpeckers. Amer. Ornithologists' Union Ornithological Monogr. No. 5, 156p.

Sherrill, D. M., and V. M. Case. 1980. Winter home ranges of four clans of red-cockaded woodpeckers in the Carolina sandhills. Wilson Bull. 92:369–375.

Tanner, J. T. 1942. The ivory-billed woodpecker. Nat. Audubon Soc. Res. Rpt. No. 1. 111 pp. Dover Publications, Inc., New York.

Chapter Eight: Bits and Pieces

Ortego, B., and D. Lay. 1988. Status of red-cockaded woodpecker colonies on private land in east Texas. Wildl. Soc. Bull. 16:403–405.

Harris, L. D. 1984. The fragmented forest. The University of Chicago Press, Chicago. 211p.

CHAPTER NINE: Beetlemania

Waters, W. E.; R. W. Stark; and D. L. Wood, eds. 1985. Integrated pest management in pine-bark beetle ecosystems. John Wiley & Sons, New York, 256 pp.

Geiszler, D. R., and others. 1980. Fire, fungi, and beetle influences on a lodgepole pine ecosystem of south-central Oregon. Oecologia 46:239–243.

CHAPTER TEN: Woodpeckers as Agents of Biological Control

McFarlane, R. W. 1976. Birds as agents of biological control. The Biologist 58(4):123–140.

Kroll, J. C.; R. N. Conner; and R. R. Fleet. 1980. Woodpeckers and the southern pine beetle. U.S. Dept. Agriculture Handbook No. 564, 23 pp.

Takekawa, J. Y.; E. O. Garton; and L. A. Langelier. 1982. Biological control of forest insect outbreaks: the use of avian predators. Trans. N. Amer. Wildlife & Nat. Resources Conference, pp. 393–409.

CHAPTER ELEVEN: Peckerwood Politics

King, W. B. and others. 1977. The recovery team-recovery plan approach to conservation of endangered species: a status summary and appraisal. American Ornithologists' Union, Report of the Committee on Conservation, 1976–77. Auk 94(4, Suppl.):1DD–19DD.

Ligon, J. D., and others. 1986. Report of the American Ornithologists' Union Committee for the Conservation of the Red-cockaded woodpecker. Auk 103(4):848–855.

Jackson, J. A. 1986. Biopolitics, management of federal lands, and the conservation of the red-cockaded woodpecker. American Birds 40(5):1162–1168.

——— and others. 1979. Recovery plan for the red-cockaded woodpecker. U.S. Fish & Wildlife Service.

Lennartz, M. R., and V. G. Henry. 1985. Endangered species recovery plan, red-cockaded woodpecker. U.S. Fish and Wildlife Service, Atlanta, Georgia, 88 pp.

CHAPTER TWELVE: Meanwhile, Deep
in the Heart of Texas . . .

Conner, R. N., and D. C. Rudolph. 1989. Red-cockaded wood-pecker colony status and trends on the Angelina, Davy Crockett, and Sabine National Forests. U.S. Dept. Agriculture, Forest Service Res. Paper SO-250, 15p.

Baker, W. W. 1983. Decline and extirpation of a population of red-cockaded woodpeckers in northwest Florida. Pp. 44–45 *in* Red-cockaded woodpecker symposium II proceedings (D. A. Wood, ed.).

Acknowledgments

Thanks are due to the hundreds of scientists whose observations and insight contribute to our body of ecological knowledge. Few scientists contribute original thoughts. Most scientists process and recycle, and perhaps reformulate, bits and pieces of information gleaned from the scientific literature and their colleagues. It is relatively easy for an author to "get credit" for nonoriginal ideas and very difficult to keep track of the origin of certain thoughts. Thus giving credit where credit is due becomes haphazard at best. I have tried to indicate the source of certain ideas expressed in this book. Where I have failed, please be assured that it is the result of the scientific process, not malice. The thoughts expressed in this book represent fifteen years of cross-fertilization and incubation.

I have learned much about the red-cockaded woodpecker from

257

the writings of those who have labored in the pineywoods to under-stand this fascinating bird. I have gleaned further knowledge from random conversations with the handful of these authors I have been privileged to know: Dick Conner, Bob Hooper, Jerry Jackson, Dan Lay, Mike Lennartz, Dave Ligon, and Jeff Walters. To all I express my gratitude for their patience and willingness to share information. I alone am responsible for any errors or misinterpreta-tions of their collective wisdom.

I am indebted to Ellen Mabry, who breathed life into some crude sketches and wisps of ideas presented to her. Her illustrations greatly enhance this story. Eric Iversen labored mightily to correct my grammatical errors, banish technical jargon, and convert my ramblings into terse prose. He did not win every battle, but if the reader has grasped the bulk of this tale, it is a attribute to Eric's diligence. We amiably disagree on the lowest common denomina-tor, polysyllabic words, and the capability of the literate lay reader.

Finally, mere words cannot express my appreciation to the Com-monwealth Fund Book Program for the opportunity to embark on this project. Without its support, and infinite patience, this story could not have been told. I, and a certain loquacious woodpecker, thank them.

Index

259

6/00